LIGHT MUFFINS

THE LOW-FAT KITCHEN

LIGHT MUFFINS

Over 60 Recipes for Sweet and Savory Low-Fat Muffins and Spreads

By Beatrice Ojakangas

Clarkson Potter/Publishers
New York

Published by Clarkson N. Potter/Publishers, 201 East 50th Street, New York, New York 10022. Member of the Crown Publishing Group.

Random House, Inc. New York, Toronto, London, Sydney, Auckland

CLARKSON N. POTTER, POTTER, and colophon are trademarks of Clarkson N. Potter, Inc.

Manufactured in the United States
Design by Renato Stanisic

Library of Congress Cataloging-in-Publication Data
Ojakangas, Beatrice A.
   Light muffins : over 60 recipes for sweet and savory low-fat muffins
and spreads / by Beatrice Ojakangas.—1st ed.
   Includes index.
   1. Muffins.   2. Low-fat diet—Recipes.   3. Low-calorie diet—
   Recipes.   I. Title.
TX770.M83053   1995
641.8'15—dc20   94-42664
                                              CIP

ISBN   0-517-70066-2

10   9   8   7   6   5   4   3   2   1

First Edition

Contents

Introduction

Muffins were always a special treat in our family. We baked up trays of them whenever the urge struck, using ripe wild blueberries in the middle of the summer, putting so many into the batter that the muffins barely held together as we ate them over our morning coffee. We would use apples in the fall, strawberries in the spring, nuts in the winter, basically whatever was on hand or was seasonal.

It was during the '80s that muffins took on a whole new identity and gained enormous popularity. Bridging the gap between bread and cake, muffins masqueraded as health food, overstuffed with fruits, nuts, and whole grains. But, underneath the oat bran and the whole wheat lurked staggering amounts of fat, sugar, and calories. And the often enormous size of these muffins made eating one muffin the caloric and fat equivalent of eating an entire cake or quick bread. As we reasoned that if a regular muffin is good for you, a bigger one must be even better, we indulged in giants weighing in at as much as 1,000 calories and containing 75 percent of their calories from fat.

So now we know better. But would a low-fat muffin be as delicious and satisfying as those fat-laden muffins of yesteryear? The answer: a resounding, a delicious yes.

All of the recipes in this book have less than 30 percent of their calories from fat, as recommended by the American Heart Association and most other major nutritional and medical organizations. I don't use any strange, hard-to-find, or artificial ingredients, and all of the muffins are quite simple and quick to put together.

I experimented with pureed fruits, substituting them for fat to provide moistness, tenderness, and flavor, the three qualities most often lacking in a low-fat baked good. Liquid sweeteners such as honey and molasses also add flavor and moistness. Another technique that ensures that these low-fat muffins won't become dry is the addition of a pro-portionately large amount of liquid to the batter. In addition, I short-ened the baking time and slightly increased the baking temperature in many of the recipes, allowing the muffins to be nicely browned on the outside yet moist inside.

I always use a flour with a low-gluten content, such as cake or all-purpose flour, which also makes for a more tender crumb. Small amounts of oil or other shortening are necessary for flavor and texture, and nut oils, such as walnut oil, are great because they provide the won-derful flavor of nuts to the muffins but add far fewer calories than would nuts themselves. Nut oils are available at gourmet and specialty shops and in the gourmet section of some supermarkets. When the crunch of nuts was called for, I just topped the muffins with a sprinkling of chopped nuts in order to save fat calories.

The muffins are divided into chapters suggesting appropriate times to enjoy them, but naturally a Banana-Chunk Muffin would be as appealing as a tea-time treat as it would for dessert.

I baked at least 300 dozen recipes while testing for this book, and after tasting the muffins myself, I usually packed them up and gave them away. In return I got feedback from my friends. The best comment came from one happy taster who said, "I don't like these muffins as well as the old kind . . . I like them better!"

BASIC LOW-FAT MUFFIN INFORMATION

Measuring

When measuring flour and other dry ingredients, stir the flour to light-en it, then spoon it into a measuring cup intended for dry goods. Level the top by sweeping a straight-edged spatula or knife across the rim. I actually keep a wooden chopstick in the flour bin to use for this purpose, as well as for stirring up flour that may have become packed.

Use a clear glass or plastic cup for measuring liquid ingredients.

Place the cup on a level surface and pour in the liquid, looking at the measurement lines at eye level.

To measure honey and molasses, coat the measuring utensil with nonstick vegetable spray so that the contents will pour out easily and completely. If the recipe calls for oil, measure the oil first so that it will coat the measuring utensil, and then measure the honey or molasses in the same utensil.

Mixing

For the most perfectly textured and shaped muffins, mix the muffin batter *just* until the dry ingredients are moistened. This usually means no more than 20 strokes of a mixing spoon or spatula. Overmixing will develop the gluten in the flour, which will cause large bubbles to form during baking, resulting in a tougher texture.

Baking

Almost all of the following muffin recipes make one dozen regular-sized muffins. A standard muffin cup holds ½ cup liquid, although some may be smaller, holding about ⅓ cup. All of the recipes in this book were baked in ½ cup-sized muffin cups. If your muffin cups are smaller, simply bake more muffins, but be sure to watch the cooking time carefully, since the muffins will probably take a few minutes less to bake. Also, note that the nutritional analysis will need adjustment for the smaller muffins.

I use an ice cream scoop to fill muffin cups. No matter what size muffin cup you use, make sure the batter is divided evenly among the cups. Sometimes the cups will be full to the top with batter, sometimes they will not be completely filled, but when baked, the tops will always be sumptuously rounded, not overflowing, producing a moist and tender product. This works especially well when the batter contains a large amount of solids, such as dried and fresh fruits.

Pay close attention to the baking time; low-fat muffins can become dry if they are baked too long. In general, the cooking times for these muffins are less than for muffins with higher fat contents.

Avoiding sticking

Baked muffins that are low in fat have a common problem: They tend to stick to paper liners. To solve this problem, either skip the paper liners and coat the muffin cups generously with nonstick baking spray, or coat the liners themselves with nonstick spray before you pour in the batter.

For mini-muffins

If you wish to make mini-muffins, spoon ⅓ as much batter into each mini-cup as you would spoon into a standard-sized baking cup. Reduce the baking time by half, but start checking the muffins a minute or two earlier than that. They are ready when a wooden skewer inserted into the middle of a muffin comes out clean. Divide the nutritional count by three.

For giant muffins

Spoon twice as much batter as needed for regular-sized baking cups into each of the giant muffin cups. You will make only half the number of muffins as you would if you used regular-sized muffin cups. Increase the baking time by 5 minutes, and test for doneness by inserting a wooden skewer into the center of a muffin and checking that it comes out clean. Double the nutritional count.

To bake muffins in a microwave oven

To bake in the microwave, line microwave-safe muffin cups or ceramic custard cups with 2 liners, then coat with nonstick spray. Fill the lined muffin cups ⅔ full with batter. If you are baking more than one muffin at a time, arrange the filled cups in a circle in the microwave. For easy handling, place them on a microwave-safe plate. Microwave at high power for 1 to 1¼ minutes for a single muffin, 2 to 2¼ minutes for 2 muffins, 2½ to 3 minutes for 4 muffins, or 3 to 3½ minutes for 6 muffins. Rotate the muffins a half turn midway through the cooking. When the muffins are done, immediately remove the muffins from the muffin cups and discard the paper liners, which will absorb some of the muffins' moisture.

Note that when muffins are baked in the microwave oven, less batter is used, and therefore the recipe yields about 25 percent more muffins. In general, the muffins should be removed from the microwave a few seconds before they look done, when the center of the top looks a bit underdone. They will continue to cook a bit after they are removed. The muffins can be returned to the microwave for a few more seconds if necessary. Each muffin will have fewer calories and fat as well.

Eggs and egg substitutes

Eggs give baked goods structure, leavening power, volume, and tenderness, and act as a binder for other ingredients in a muffin recipe. Egg yolks add certain qualities of tenderness and browning to baked goods. They also are high in cholesterol and fat. To decrease the cholesterol and fat from egg yolks in muffins, you can use either ¼ to ⅓ cup fat-free egg product or 2 egg whites in place of each egg called for in a recipe. Fat-free commercial egg products such as Egg Beaters, Simply Eggs, or Better'n Eggs are composed mainly of egg whites, with additional ingredients added to replicate the qualities of egg yolks. These products are also cholesterol-free, as are egg whites.

When I tested my muffins with egg substitutes, there were differences since I *was* further reducing the fat content. The muffins had a slightly coarser texture and did not brown as well as those made with whole egg, but they tasted good. Don't try to achieve a browner top by increasing the baking time. This will make the muffins dry. Also worth noting is that egg substitutes cost about three times as much as raw eggs, but they are very convenient.

Nutritional analysis

Unless otherwise stated, the nutritional analysis for each muffin is accurate for the first ingredient option given in the ingredient list, such as for one whole egg rather than the alternative two egg whites. However, most of the ingredient options will not alter the nutritional analysis, such as the choice between melted butter or oil, or nonfat buttermilk or water mixed with buttermilk powder.

Basic Low-Fat Muffins

From this basic recipe you can create your own customized muffins by substituting different flours and adding fruits, spices, and other fat-free or low-fat flavorings. These muffins are not only low in fat, falling within the recommended guideline of providing 30 percent of their calories from fat, but also low in sugar. These muffins are slightly sweet, tender, and a bit coarse in texture, with a pebbly, browned top and an even shape. Using cake flour will result in a more tender muffin, but it does not alter the nutritional count, and if you use 2 large egg whites instead of a whole egg, the fat balance will be reduced to 28 percent calories from fat.

2 cups sifted cake or
    all-purpose flour
3 tablespoons sugar
3 teaspoons baking powder
½ teaspoon salt
1 cup skim milk

1 large egg, lightly beaten, or
    2 large egg whites, lightly
    beaten
4 tablespoons (½ stick) melted
    unsalted butter or vegetable
    oil

Preheat the oven to 400° F. Lightly grease or coat with nonstick spray 12 regular-sized muffin cups, or line with paper baking cups.

In a large bowl, stir together the flour, sugar, baking powder, and salt. In a small bowl, mix the milk, egg, and melted butter or oil. Stir the liquid ingredients into the dry ingredients just until blended, about 20 strokes.

Spoon the batter into the muffin cups. Bake for 15 to 20 minutes, or until the muffins are lightly browned and a wooden skewer inserted into the center of the muffin comes out clean. Cool 1 minute, then remove from the muffin tins and transfer to a wire rack to cool or to a basket to serve warm.

Makes 12 muffins

PER MUFFIN: 136 cal. (30% from fat), 4.5 g. fat, 0.5 g. fiber

Variations that will not increase the percent of calories from fat

SWEETENERS: *For sweeter muffins,* increase the sugar up to ½ cup. *For brown sugar muffins,* use up to ½ cup brown sugar in place of the white sugar, mixing it with the dry ingredients. *For honey muffins,* add up to ½ cup honey in place of the sugar, mixing the honey with the liquid rather than the dry ingredients.

FLOURS: *For whole wheat muffins,* substitute whole wheat flour for half or all of the all-purpose flour. *For cornmeal muffins,* substitute cornmeal for up to half of the all-purpose flour. *For multi-grain muffins,* substitute rolled oats, rye flour, triticale, or any other whole grain flour or a mixture of several flours for half of the all-purpose flour. Or you may substitute 2 tablespoons of unprocessed bran, wheat germ, or buckwheat flour for the all-purpose flour.

FRUITS: Add to the batter ½ to 1 cup dried or fresh fruits such as chopped apples, pears, apricots, peaches, raisins, prunes, dates, cherries, blueberries, or strawberries.

OTHER FLAVORINGS: Add ½ teaspoon dried herbs, up to 3 teaspoons chopped fresh herbs, ½ teaspoon ground spices (such as cardamom, cinnamon, nutmeg, cloves, allspice, or coriander), or ½ to 1 teaspoon grated citrus zest (such as orange, lemon, lime, or grapefruit) to the dry ingredients.

Breakfast and Brunch Muffins

Breakfast Apple Muffins

Rolled oats ground into a flour make these muffins exceptionally tender and nutritious. Hazelnut oil is available in the gourmet section of many supermarkets, although melted butter adds a delicious flavor, too.

2 cups uncooked quick rolled oats
½ cup all-purpose flour
2 tablespoons whole wheat flour
½ cup packed brown sugar
2 teaspoons baking powder
½ teaspoon baking soda
½ teaspoon salt
1½ teaspoons ground cinnamon
¼ teaspoon ground nutmeg
¼ cup dried currants

1 cup nonfat buttermilk
3 large egg whites
1 tablespoon hazelnut oil or
    unsalted butter, melted
3 tablespoons corn oil
1 teaspoon vanilla extract
1 large Granny Smith apple,
    peeled, cored, and cut into
    ¼-inch dice
1 tablespoon sugar

Preheat the oven to 400° F. Lightly grease 12 regular-sized muffin cups, or coat with nonstick spray.

Measure the rolled oats into the container of a blender or into a food processor with the steel blade in place. Process or blend until the oats are finely ground.

In a large bowl, stir together the oat flour, all-purpose flour, whole wheat flour, brown sugar, baking powder, baking soda, salt, cinnamon, nutmeg, and currants. In a small bowl, mix the buttermilk, egg whites, hazelnut oil or butter, corn oil, and vanilla. Stir the liquid ingredients into the dry ingredients until almost blended, about 20 strokes. Gently stir in the apple until evenly mixed into the batter.

Spoon the batter into the muffin cups, dividing the batter evenly. Sprinkle the tops of the muffins with the 1 tablespoon sugar. Bake for 20 to 25 minutes, or until the muffins are lightly browned and a wooden skewer inserted in the center of a muffin comes out clean. Cool 1 minute, then remove from the muffin tin and transfer to a wire rack to cool or to a basket to serve warm.

Makes 12 muffins

PER MUFFIN (WITH OIL): 178 cal. (30% from fat), 6 g. fat, 2 g. fiber

Cornmeal~Pineapple Muffins

Crushed pineapple in the batter and a surprise pocket of pineapple preserves in the center make these muffins moist and flavorful.

1½ cups all-purpose flour
1 cup yellow cornmeal
2 tablespoons sugar
4 teaspoons baking powder
½ teaspoon salt
2 large eggs, lightly beaten
1¼ cups skim milk

4 tablespoons (½ stick) unsalted
  butter, melted
½ cup well-drained canned
  crushed pineapple
6 tablespoons pineapple jam or
  preserves

Preheat the oven to 400° F. Lightly grease 12 regular-sized muffin cups, or 36 miniature cups, or coat with nonstick spray.

In a large bowl, thoroughly mix the flour, cornmeal, sugar, baking powder, and salt. In a small bowl, whisk together the eggs, milk, butter, and pineapple. Add the liquid ingredients to the dry ingredients and stir just until the dry ingredients are moistened, about 20 strokes. Spoon 2 tablespoons of the batter into each regular-sized muffin cup, or 2 teaspoons of the batter into each miniature cup. Drop ½ teaspoon of the pineapple jam or preserves into the center of each larger muffin, or a tiny bit into the mini-muffins. Divide the remaining batter evenly among the muffin cups to cover the preserves. Bake for 15 to 20 minutes for regular-sized muffins, or 10 to 15 minutes for miniature muffins, or until a wooden skewer inserted in a muffin slightly off center comes out clean. Let the muffins cool in the tin for about 3 minutes, remove, and cool on a rack or transfer to a basket to serve warm.

Makes 12 regular-sized muffins or 36 mini-muffins

PER MUFFIN: 182 cal. (25% from fat), 5 g. fat, 1.4 g. fiber

Dried Cranberry-Raisin Grain Muffins

Tart dried cranberries look like crimson raisins and can be found bulk packaged in the produce department of the supermarket, or at specialty or health-food stores.

1 cup all-purpose flour
¾ cup whole wheat flour
1 cup uncooked old-fashioned
   rolled oats
½ cup packed brown sugar
½ cup dry Grape-Nuts cereal
4 teaspoons baking powder
½ teaspoon salt

2 teaspoons ground cinnamon
½ cup dried cranberries
½ cup dark or golden raisins
1 cup skim milk
3 tablespoons unsalted butter,
   melted
2 large eggs, lightly beaten, or 3
   large egg whites, lightly beaten

Preheat the oven to 400° F. Lightly grease 12 regular-sized muffin cups, or coat with nonstick spray.

In a large bowl, mix the flours, rolled oats, brown sugar, Grape-Nuts, baking powder, salt, cinnamon, dried cranberries, and raisins. Make a well in the center of the dry ingredients and add the milk, butter, and eggs or egg whites. Stir the mixture just until blended, about 20 strokes.

Spoon the batter into the muffin cups, dividing the batter evenly. Bake for 17 to 20 minutes, or until the muffins are lightly browned and a wooden skewer inserted into the center of a muffin comes out clean. Cool 1 minute, then remove from the muffin tin and transfer to a wire rack to cool or to a basket to serve warm.

Makes 12 muffins

PER MUFFIN (WITH 2 EGGS): 200 cal. (about 16% from fat),
3.5 g. fat, 3 g. fiber

Glorious Morning Muffins

Replacing most of the oil with applesauce makes an equally tasty muffin.

1 cup all-purpose flour
¾ cup whole wheat flour
¼ cup dry Grape-Nuts cereal
¾ cup packed brown sugar
2 teaspoons baking powder
1 teaspoon baking soda
½ teaspoon salt
1 tablespoon ground cinnamon
2 cups grated peeled carrots
1 apple, such as Granny Smith, peeled, cored, and chopped

1 cup raisins
1 large egg, lightly beaten
2 large egg whites, lightly beaten
½ cup unsweetened applesauce
¼ cup safflower or corn oil
1 tablespoon vanilla extract
1 tablespoon finely chopped walnuts
1 tablespoon wheat germ

Preheat the oven to 400° F. Lightly grease 12 regular-sized muffin cups, or coat with nonstick spray.

In a large bowl, mix the flours, Grape-Nuts, sugar, baking powder, baking soda, salt, cinnamon, carrots, apple, and raisins. Make a well in the center of the dry ingredients and add the egg, egg whites, applesauce, oil, and vanilla. Stir just until blended, about 20 strokes.

Spoon the batter into the muffin cups, dividing the batter evenly. Sprinkle with the nuts and wheat germ. Bake for 17 to 20 minutes, or until the muffins are lightly browned and a wooden skewer inserted in the center of a muffin comes out clean. Cool 1 minute, then remove from the muffin tin and transfer to a wire rack to cool or to a basket to serve warm.

Makes 12 muffins

PER MUFFIN: 230 cal. (22% from fat), 5 g. fat, 3 g. fiber

Apple-Cheddar Muffins

I've always loved the flavor of apple pie served with cheddar cheese, so I put these two ingredients together in a muffin.

1½ cups all-purpose flour
½ cup whole wheat flour
½ cup sugar
3 teaspoons baking powder
¼ teaspoon salt
½ teaspoon ground cinnamon

1½ cups chopped peeled tart apples, such as Granny Smith
1 cup shredded cheddar cheese
1 cup skim milk
2 tablespoons (¼ stick) unsalted butter, melted
1 large egg, lightly beaten

Preheat the oven to 400° F. Lightly grease 12 regular-sized muffin cups, or coat with nonstick spray.

In a large bowl, mix the flours, sugar, baking powder, salt, and cinnamon. Add the chopped apples and the cheese and mix gently until the apple and cheese are evenly distributed in the flour mixture. In a small bowl, stir together the milk, melted butter, and egg. Stir the liquid ingredients into the dry ingredients just until blended, about 20 to 25 strokes.

Spoon the batter into the muffin cups, dividing the batter evenly. Bake for 20 to 25 minutes, or until the muffins are lightly browned and a wooden skewer inserted in the center of a muffin comes out clean. Cool 1 minute, then remove from the muffin tin and transfer to a wire rack to cool or to a basket to serve warm.

Makes 12 muffins

PER MUFFIN: 179 cal. (29% from fat), 6 g. fat, 1.3 g. fiber

Hazelnut-Pear Muffins

To make the most of the flavor and texture of filberts (hazelnuts), I use them as a topping for these muffins. To further enhance the flavor, I use hazelnut oil, which I buy in my favorite gourmet shop.

2 cups all-purpose flour
1/4 cup whole wheat flour
3 teaspoons baking powder
1/2 teaspoon salt
1 teaspoon grated lemon zest
1 large ripe pear, peeled, seeded, and diced

3/4 cup skim milk
4 tablespoons hazelnut or corn oil
1/3 cup honey
2 large egg whites, lightly beaten
2 tablespoons chopped hazelnuts (filberts)

Preheat the oven to 400° F. Lightly grease 12 regular-sized muffin cups, or coat with nonstick spray.

In a large bowl, mix the all-purpose flour, whole wheat flour, baking powder, salt, and lemon zest. Fold in the diced pear until the pear pieces are coated. In a small bowl, beat the milk, oil, honey, and egg whites together. Stir the liquid ingredients into the dry ingredients just until blended, about 20 strokes.

Spoon the batter into the muffin cups, dividing the batter evenly. Sprinkle the tops of the muffins with the hazelnuts. Lightly press the nuts into the batter. Bake for 20 to 25 minutes, or until the muffins are lightly browned and a wooden skewer inserted in the center of a muffin comes out clean. Cool 1 minute, then remove from the muffin tin and transfer to a wire rack to cool or to a basket to serve warm.

Makes 12 muffins

PER MUFFIN: 158 cal. (28% from fat), 5 g. fat, 1 g. fiber

Hot-Cross Muffins

These are a muffin version of the classic hot-cross buns that are traditionally served on Good Friday.

½ cup dark or golden raisins
2 cups sifted cake flour
½ cup sugar
2 teaspoons baking powder
½ teaspoon baking soda
¼ teaspoon salt
3 tablespoons unsalted butter, melted

2 large eggs, lightly beaten
1 cup nonfat plain yogurt
1 teaspoon grated orange zest

FROSTING
½ cup confectioners' sugar
½ teaspoon vanilla extract
1 to 2 tablespoons milk

In a small bowl add hot water to cover the raisins. Let stand for 1 minute, then drain well. Preheat the oven to 400° F. Lightly grease 12 regular-sized muffin cups, or coat with nonstick spray.

In a large bowl, stir the flour, sugar, baking powder, baking soda, salt, and raisins together. In a small bowl, mix the butter, eggs, yogurt, and orange zest together. Stir the liquid ingredients into the dry ingredients just until the dry ingredients are moistened.

Spoon the batter into the muffin cups, dividing the batter evenly. Bake for 18 to 20 minutes, until golden or a wooden skewer inserted in the center of a muffin comes out clean. Cool 1 minute, then remove from the muffin tin and transfer to a wire rack to cool.

To make the frosting, in a small bowl stir together the confectioners' sugar, vanilla, and enough milk to make a smooth frosting. Drizzle the frosting onto each muffin to make a cross.

Makes 12 muffins

PER MUFFIN: 194 cal. (19% from fat), 3.95 g. fat, 1.17 g. fiber

Oat-Cranberry Muffins

Cranberries provide a tart bite to these delicious muffins, which are perfect for an autumn breakfast or brunch. If you use frozen cranberries, you can add them to the batter without defrosting them, but expect the muffins to take up to 5 minutes longer to bake.

¾ cup all-purpose flour
¾ cup whole wheat flour
1 cup old-fashioned uncooked
    rolled oats
½ cup packed brown sugar
3 teaspoons baking powder
½ teaspoon salt

1 teaspoon ground cinnamon
1 cup fresh or frozen whole
    cranberries
1 cup skim milk
3 tablespoons unsalted butter,
    melted
1 large egg, lightly beaten

Preheat the oven to 400° F. Lightly grease 12 regular-sized muffin cups, or coat with nonstick spray.

In a large bowl, mix the flours, rolled oats, brown sugar, baking powder, salt, cinnamon, and cranberries. In a small bowl, beat the milk, butter, and egg together. Stir the liquid ingredients into the dry ingredients just until blended, about 20 strokes.

Spoon the batter into the muffin cups, dividing the batter evenly. Bake for 20 to 25 minutes, or until the muffins are lightly browned and a wooden skewer inserted in the center of a muffin comes out clean. Cool 1 minute, then remove from the muffin tin and transfer to a wire rack to cool or to a basket to serve warm.

Makes 12 muffins

PER MUFFIN: 165 cal. (25% from fat), 4 g. fat, 2 g. fiber

Oat – Whole Wheat Banana Muffins

Low in fat and high in fiber, these muffins are almost a whole breakfast in themselves.

1½ cups uncooked quick rolled oats
1½ cups whole wheat flour
⅓ cup packed brown sugar
3 teaspoons baking powder
½ teaspoon ground cinnamon
¼ teaspoon ground ginger
¼ teaspoon salt

1 cup fresh or dried blueberries (optional)
1 cup skim milk
½ cup (1 medium) mashed ripe banana
2 tablespoons walnut or corn oil
1 large egg, beaten

Preheat the oven to 400° F. Lightly grease 12 regular-sized muffin cups, or coat with nonstick spray.

In a large bowl, thoroughly mix the rolled oats with the whole wheat flour, brown sugar, baking powder, cinnamon, ginger, and salt. Add the blueberries, if using, and stir gently until the berries are evenly distributed in the mixture. In a small bowl, stir together the milk, banana, oil, and egg until blended. Add the liquid ingredients to the dry ingredients and stir just until the dry ingredients are moistened, about 20 strokes.

Spoon the batter into the muffin cups, dividing the batter evenly. Bake for 15 to 20 minutes, or until a wooden skewer inserted in the center of a muffin comes out clean. Cool the muffins in the tin for 3 minutes, remove, and cool on a rack or transfer to a basket to serve warm.

Makes 12 muffins

PER MUFFIN: 154 cal. (21% from fat), 3 g. fat, 3 g. fiber

Orange and Prune Muffins

A bit of sugar sprinkled on top of these muffins before baking gives them a crunchy top. Break open a hot-from-the-oven muffin and catch the aroma of orange. Serve them with a purchased nonfat fruit-flavored cream cheese.

2 cups all-purpose flour
½ cup plus 1 tablespoon sugar
3 teaspoons baking powder
½ teaspoon salt
2 teaspoons grated orange zest
1 cup chopped prunes

4 tablespoons (½ stick) unsalted butter, melted, or 4 tablespoons vegetable oil
1 large egg, lightly beaten
1 cup skim milk

Preheat the oven to 400° F. Lightly grease 12 regular-sized muffin cups, or coat with nonstick spray.

In a large bowl, stir the flour, ½ cup sugar, baking powder, salt, orange zest, and prunes together. In a small bowl, mix the butter or oil, egg, and skim milk until blended. Stir the liquid ingredients into the dry ingredients just until the dry ingredients are moistened, about 20 strokes.

Spoon the batter into the muffin cups, dividing the batter evenly. Sprinkle the tops of the muffins with the remaining 1 tablespoon sugar. Bake for 20 to 25 minutes, until the muffins are light golden brown or until a wooden skewer inserted in the center of a muffin comes out clean. Remove the muffins from the tin and place them in a basket to serve warm.

Makes 12 muffins

PER MUFFIN: 180 cal. (23% from fat), 4 g. fat, 1.5 g. fiber

Wild Rice and
Blueberry Muffins

Wild rice adds a chewy texture to these muffins, but you should make sure the rice is very well cooked or it will be hard and crunchy. I store extra cooked wild rice in plastic bags in the freezer so that I can have it on hand to add to muffins, breads, and soups.

1½ cups all-purpose flour
½ cup sugar
3 teaspoons baking powder
1 teaspoon ground coriander
    seeds
½ teaspoon salt

1 cup cooked wild rice
1 cup fresh blueberries, dried
    blueberries, or raisins
4 tablespoons corn oil
1 large egg, beaten
½ cup skim milk

Preheat the oven to 400° F. Lightly grease 12 regular-sized muffin cups, or coat with nonstick spray.

In a large bowl, mix the flour, sugar, baking powder, coriander, salt, wild rice, and blueberries or raisins. In a small bowl, beat the oil, egg, and milk together. Stir the liquid ingredients into the dry ingredients just until blended, about 20 strokes.

Spoon the batter into the muffin cups, dividing the batter evenly. Bake for 20 to 25 minutes, or until the muffins are lightly browned and a wooden skewer inserted in the center of a muffin comes out clean. Cool 1 minute, then remove from the muffin tin and transfer to a wire rack to cool or to a basket to serve warm.

Makes 12 muffins

PER MUFFIN: 160 cal. (29% from fat), 5 g. fat, 1 g. fiber

Orange-Glazed Whole Wheat Muffins

These flavorful and light muffins are just wonderful hot out of the oven. But the orange glaze keeps them moist, so they are just as delicious the next day.

¾ cup whole wheat flour
½ cup sugar
1 cup all-purpose flour
½ teaspoon baking powder
½ teaspoon baking soda
¼ teaspoon salt
1 cup nonfat lemon yogurt
⅓ cup vegetable or corn oil

2 teaspoons grated orange zest
1 tablespoon lemon juice
1 large egg, beaten
2 tablespoons orange marmalade

ORANGE GLAZE
3 tablespoons sugar
3 tablespoons orange juice

Preheat the oven to 400° F. Lightly grease 12 regular-sized muffin cups, or coat with nonstick spray.

In a large bowl, stir together the whole wheat flour and sugar. Add the all-purpose flour, baking powder, baking soda, and salt and mix well. In a small bowl, stir together the yogurt, oil, orange zest, lemon juice, and egg. Add the liquid ingredients to the dry ingredients and stir just until blended, about 20 strokes. Spoon the batter into the muffin cups, dividing the batter evenly. Make an indentation in the center of each cup of batter and spoon ½ teaspoon of the marmalade onto each muffin.

Bake for 18 to 20 minutes, or until golden brown or a wooden skewer inserted in a muffin just off center comes out clean.

To make the glaze, while the muffins bake, combine the sugar and orange juice in a small pan. Bring to a boil over medium heat. Stir until the sugar is dissolved. As soon as the muffins are done, brush the tops of the muffins with the glaze, brushing each muffin several times until all the glaze is used. Cool in the tin for 5 minutes. Remove from the muffin tin, then transfer to a wire rack or to a basket to serve warm.

Makes 12 muffins

PER MUFFIN: 210 cal. (27% from fat), 6 g. fat, 1.3 g. fiber

Seven-Grain Muffins

In my local whole-foods cooperative, I buy a cereal composed of seven different cracked grains: wheat, oats, triticale, buckwheat, rye, corn, and millet. You can use any similarly textured multigrain cereal, from simple cracked wheat to various grain combinations of four to nine grains, to make these muffins. Cracked grains need to be softened, but not completely cooked, before using.

½ cup seven-grain cereal
¾ cup boiling water
2 cups all-purpose flour
2 teaspoons baking powder
1 teaspoon baking soda

1 teaspoon salt
¾ cup buttermilk
⅓ cup honey
1 large egg, lightly beaten

Measure the seven-grain cereal into a small bowl and pour the boiling water over. Let it stand 10 minutes, or just until the cereal has softened. Drain off any excess water.

Preheat the oven to 400° F. Lightly grease 12 regular-sized muffin cups, or coat with nonstick spray.

In a large bowl, stir the flour, baking powder, baking soda, and salt together. Add the buttermilk, honey, and egg to the soaked cereal and stir to blend.

Add the liquid ingredients to the dry ingredients and stir just until combined, about 20 strokes. Spoon the batter into the muffin cups, dividing the batter evenly. Bake for 20 to 25 minutes, or until a wooden skewer inserted in the center of a muffin comes out clean. Cool 1 minute, then remove from the muffin tin and transfer to a wire rack to cool or to a basket to serve warm.

Makes 12 muffins

PER MUFFIN: 163 cal. (28% from fat), 5 g. fat, 0.6 g. fiber

Snack
Muffins

Almond‑Strawberry Muffins

Strawberries baked into these muffins provide a tart, fruity flavor burst. I use large strawberries that are ripe but firm enough to cut into ⅓-inch dice. Almonds sprinkled on top toast as the muffins bake, providing texture and flavor.

2 cups sifted cake flour or
    all‑purpose flour
¼ cup whole wheat flour
3 teaspoons baking powder
½ teaspoon salt
1 teaspoon grated lemon zest
1½ cups diced fresh strawberries
¾ cup skim milk

4 tablespoons canola oil, or 4
    tablespoons (½ stick) unsalted
    butter, melted
⅓ cup honey
2 large egg whites, lightly beaten
2 tablespoons chopped blanched
    almonds

Preheat the oven to 400° F. Lightly grease 12 regular-sized muffin cups, or coat with nonstick spray.

In a large bowl, mix the cake flour or all-purpose flour, whole wheat flour, baking powder, salt, and lemon zest. Fold in the diced strawberries. In a small bowl, beat the milk, oil or butter, honey, and egg whites together. Stir the liquid ingredients into the dry ingredients just until blended, about 20 strokes.

Spoon the batter into the muffin cups, dividing the batter evenly. Sprinkle the tops of the muffins with the nuts. Lightly press the nuts into the batter. Bake for 20 to 25 minutes, or until the muffins are lightly browned and a wooden skewer inserted in the center of the muffin comes out clean. Cool 1 minute, then remove from the muffin tin and transfer to a wire rack to cool or to a basket to serve warm.

Makes 12 muffins

PER MUFFIN: 158 cal. (28% from fat), 5 g. fat, 1 g. fiber

Carrot~Raisin Muffins

Sometimes when we have company, I make this muffin batter the night before so that we can have fresh hot muffins for breakfast without any fuss. After mixing the batter, I just spoon it into the muffin tin, cover the whole pan with plastic wrap, and refrigerate it overnight. All that's necessary in the morning is to preheat the oven and bake them. The muffins are wonderful served with slightly softened nonfat or low-fat cream cheese.

1½ cups all-purpose flour
½ cup sugar
1½ teaspoons baking powder
½ teaspoon salt
1½ cups grated peeled carrots

½ cup dark or golden raisins
3 large egg whites, lightly beaten
3 tablespoons walnut, hazelnut, or corn oil
½ cup skim milk

Preheat the oven to 400° F. Lightly grease 12 regular-sized muffin cups, or coat with nonstick spray.

In a large bowl, stir together the flour, sugar, baking powder, and salt. Add the carrots and raisins and mix until the carrots and raisins are evenly blended into the dry ingredients. In a small bowl, mix the egg whites, oil, and milk. Stir the liquid ingredients into the dry ingredients just until blended, about 25 strokes.

Spoon the batter into the muffin cups, dividing the batter evenly. Bake for 20 to 25 minutes, or until the muffins are lightly browned and a wooden skewer inserted into the center of a muffin comes out clean. Cool 1 minute, then remove from the muffin tin and transfer to a wire rack to cool or to a basket to serve warm.

Makes 12 muffins

PER MUFFIN: 166 cal. (29% from fat), 5.5 g. fat, 1.19 g. fiber

Banana Crunch–Top Muffins

Wheat germ in the muffin batter and in the topping adds a satisfying crunch to these muffins. A perennial favorite with kids and adults alike, banana muffins are wonderful for breakfast, either by themselves or with cereal, eggs, or whatever you're in the mood for!

1½ cups all-purpose flour
½ cup wheat germ
½ cup packed brown sugar
3 teaspoons baking powder
1 teaspoon ground cinnamon
¼ teaspoon ground nutmeg
½ teaspoon salt
2 medium ripe bananas, mashed
  (about ¾ cup)
¾ cup skim milk
3 tablespoons unsalted butter,
  melted

2 large egg whites, lightly beaten

WHEAT GERM TOPPING I
3 tablespoons wheat germ
2 tablespoons packed brown
  sugar
1 tablespoon all-purpose flour
1 tablespoon unsalted butter,
  melted
⅛ teaspoon ground cinnamon

Preheat the oven to 400° F. Lightly grease 12 regular-sized muffin cups, or coat with nonstick spray.

In a large mixing bowl, combine the flour, wheat germ, brown sugar, baking powder, cinnamon, nutmeg, and salt.

In a small bowl, mix together the mashed bananas, milk, butter, and egg whites. Stir the liquid ingredients into the dry ingredients just until the dry ingredients are moistened, about 20 strokes.

Spoon the batter into the muffin cups, dividing the batter evenly.

For the wheat germ topping, in a small bowl, combine all of the topping ingredients and mix until blended. Sprinkle over the muffins, dividing the mixture equally, and pat down gently onto the muffins. Bake for 20 to 22 minutes, or until the muffins are browned and a wooden skewer inserted in the center of a muffin comes out clean. Cool 1 minute, then remove from the muffin tin and transfer to a wire rack to cool or to a basket to serve warm.

Makes 12 muffins

PER MUFFIN: 182 cal. (23% from fat), 4 g. fat, 1.6 g. fiber

Chocolate Chip–Raisin Muffins

Bake these in miniature-muffin cups to please kids and guests, who will love their crispy, browned edges. Baked in regular-sized muffin cups, they're moist and delicious.

2 cups all-purpose flour
½ cup sugar
3 teaspoons baking powder
½ teaspoon salt
½ cup dark or golden raisins
1 cup skim milk
1 large egg white, lightly beaten

4 tablespoons (½ stick) unsalted butter, melted, or 4 tablespoons corn oil
¼ cup miniature semisweet chocolate chips

Preheat the oven to 400° F. Lightly grease 12 regular-sized muffin cups, or coat with nonstick spray.

In a large bowl, stir the flour, sugar, baking powder, and salt together until well blended. Add the raisins; stir until they are evenly distributed in the flour mixture. In a small bowl, mix the milk, egg white, and butter or oil until blended. Stir the liquid ingredients into the dry ingredients just until the dry ingredients are moistened, about 20 strokes.

Spoon the mixture into the muffin cups, dividing the batter evenly. Sprinkle the tops of the muffins with the chocolate chips. Bake for 20 to 25 minutes, until light golden brown or a wooden skewer inserted in the center of a muffin comes out clean. Cool 1 minute, then remove from the muffin tin and transfer to a wire rack to cool, or to a basket to serve warm.

Makes 12 muffins

PER MUFFIN: 196 cal. (27% from fat), 6 g. fat, 1 g. fiber

Date and Nut Muffins

This great snack muffin is perfect for breakfast or brunch, as well as for an accompaniment to a chicken or seafood salad for lunch or supper.

2 cups all-purpose flour
½ cup sugar
3 teaspoons baking powder
½ teaspoon salt
1 cup chopped dates

1 cup skim milk
1 large egg, lightly beaten
4 tablespoons (½ stick) unsalted
    butter, melted
¼ cup finely chopped walnuts

Preheat the oven to 400° F. Lightly grease 12 regular-sized muffin cups, or coat with nonstick spray.

In a large bowl, stir the flour, sugar, baking powder, salt, and dates together. In a small bowl, mix the milk, egg, and butter until blended. Stir the liquid ingredients into the dry ingredients just until the dry ingredients are moistened, about 20 strokes.

Spoon the batter into the muffin cups, dividing the batter evenly. Sprinkle the tops of the muffins with the chopped nuts, dividing them equally among the muffins. Bake for 20 to 25 minutes, until light golden brown or until a wooden skewer inserted in the center of a muffin comes out clean. Cool 1 minute, then remove from the muffin tin and transfer to a wire rack to cool or to a basket to serve warm.

Makes 12 muffins

PER MUFFIN: 213 cal. (25% from fat), 6 g. fat, 1.9 g. fiber

Dried-Fruit Streusel Muffins

I've made these muffins with combinations of all sorts of dried fruits, like blueberries, cranberries, strawberries, cherries, dates, figs, raisins, and chopped dried-fruit mixtures, depending on what I have on hand. This recipe makes a large volume of muffin batter, and you can heap the muffin cups full without worrying about them running over during baking. Alternatively, you can divide the dough into 18 muffin cups for a shorter muffin.

1½ cups all-purpose flour
½ cup whole wheat flour
½ cup sugar
2 teaspoons baking powder
½ teaspoon baking soda
½ teaspoon salt
1½ cups chopped mixed dried
 fruits or dried berries
1½ cups nonfat vanilla yogurt
1 tablespoon walnut oil or
 unsalted butter, melted
2 tablespoons safflower or corn oil

2 teaspoons vanilla extract
1 large egg, lightly beaten

STREUSEL TOPPING I
⅓ cup packed brown sugar
¼ cup uncooked old-fashioned or
 quick rolled oats
2 tablespoons finely chopped
 walnuts
1 tablespoon walnut oil or
 unsalted butter, melted
¼ teaspoon ground cinnamon

Preheat the oven to 400° F. Lightly grease 12 to 18 regular-sized muffin cups, or coat with nonstick spray.

In a mixing bowl, stir together the all-purpose flour, whole wheat flour, sugar, baking powder, baking soda, and salt until well blended. Stir in the dried fruits or berries until evenly blended.

In a smaller bowl, mix the yogurt, walnut oil or butter, safflower or corn oil, vanilla, and egg until well mixed. Stir the liquid ingredients into the dry ingredients just until blended, about 20 strokes; do not overmix. Spoon the mixture into the muffin cups, dividing the batter evenly.

To make the streusel topping, in another bowl, stir the brown sugar, oats, walnuts, oil or butter, and cinnamon together. Sprinkle the streusel mixture over the muffins and gently pat it down onto the top of the batter.

Bake for 20 to 25 minutes, until a wooden skewer inserted in the center of a muffin comes out clean and dry. Cool 1 minute, then remove from the muffin tin and transfer to a wire rack to cool or to a basket to serve warm.

Makes 12 to 18 muffins

PER MUFFIN (12 muffins): 297 cal. (18% from fat), 6 g. fat, 2.5 g. fiber

PER MUFFIN (18 muffins): 198 cal. (18% from fat), 4 g. fat, 1.6 g. fiber

Fresh Peach Streusel Muffins

Chopped fresh, ripe peaches are luscious baked into these dessertlike muffins.

2 cups all-purpose flour
¼ cup whole wheat flour
3 teaspoons baking powder
½ teaspoon salt
½ cup sugar
1 large egg, lightly beaten
3 tablespoons walnut, hazelnut, or corn oil
2 teaspoons vanilla extract
1 cup chopped, peeled peaches
1 cup nonfat vanilla yogurt

STREUSEL TOPPING II
⅓ cup packed brown sugar
¼ cup uncooked old-fashioned or quick rolled oats
2 tablespoons finely chopped pecans
1 tablespoon walnut, hazelnut, or corn oil
¼ teaspoon ground cinnamon

Preheat the oven to 400° F. Lightly grease 18 regular-sized muffin cups, or coat with nonstick spray.

In a large bowl, mix the flours, baking powder, salt, and sugar. In a medium bowl, mix the egg, oil, vanilla, peaches, and yogurt. Stir the liquid ingredients into the dry ingredients until blended, about 20 strokes. Spoon the mixture into the muffin cups, dividing it evenly.

To make the topping, in a small bowl, stir the brown sugar, oats, pecans, oil, and cinnamon until the mixture resembles moist crumbs. Sprinkle the topping over the muffins and gently pat it onto the tops. Bake for 20 to 25 minutes, until a wooden skewer inserted in the center of a muffin comes out clean. Cool 1 minute, then remove from the tin and transfer to a rack to cool or a basket to serve warm.

Makes 18 muffins

PER MUFFIN: 161 cal. (23% from fat), 4 g. fat, 1 g. fiber

Orange-Cranberry Muffins

These crunchy, slightly tart muffins are reminiscent of one of my favorite Christmas quick breads.

2 cups all-purpose flour
½ cup wheat germ
3 teaspoons baking powder
½ teaspoon salt
⅔ cup plus 1 tablespoon sugar
4 teaspoons grated orange zest
1 cup fresh cranberries, coarsely chopped

4 tablespoons (½ stick) unsalted butter, melted, or 4 tablespoons walnut oil or corn oil
2 large egg whites, lightly beaten
¾ cup orange juice
2 tablespoons finely chopped walnuts

Preheat the oven to 400° F. Lightly grease 12 regular-sized muffin cups, or coat with nonstick spray.

In a large bowl, thoroughly mix the flour, wheat germ, baking powder, and salt. Stir in the ⅔ cup sugar, orange zest, and cranberries. In a small bowl, whisk together the butter or oil, egg whites, and orange juice. Add the liquid ingredients to the dry ingredients and stir just until the dry ingredients are moistened, about 20 strokes.

Spoon the batter into the muffin cups, dividing the batter evenly. Sprinkle the tops of the muffins evenly with the walnuts and the remaining 1 tablespoon sugar. Press the nuts and sugar down lightly onto the top of the batter. Bake for 20 to 25 minutes, or until a wooden skewer inserted in the center of a muffin comes out clean. Let the muffins cool in the tin for about 2 minutes, then remove and cool on a rack or transfer to a basket to serve warm.

Makes 12 muffins

PER MUFFIN: 195 cal. (24% from fat), 5 g. fat, 1.6 g. fiber

Sweet Potato
Streusel Muffins

The crunchy streusel topping and the spicy and slightly sweet flavor of these muffins make them a perfect candidate for a morning coffee party. If you mash the sweet potatoes using a hand mixer, the mixture will have tiny pieces of potato in it that add flecks of orange color and delightful moistness.

2 cups all-purpose flour
½ cup sugar
1 tablespoon baking powder
1 teaspoon ground nutmeg
1 teaspoon ground cardamom
½ teaspoon salt
1 cup mashed cooked sweet
    potatoes or yams
½ cup skim milk
2 large eggs, beaten

3 tablespoons unsalted butter,
    melted

STREUSEL TOPPING III
2 tablespoons brown sugar
2 tablespoons all-purpose flour
¼ teaspoon ground cinnamon
1 tablespoon unsalted butter, at
    room temperature

Preheat the oven to 400° F. Lightly grease 12 regular-sized muffin cups, or coat with nonstick spray.

In a large bowl, mix the flour, sugar, baking powder, nutmeg, cardamom, and salt until well blended.

In a medium bowl, mash the sweet potatoes or yams until coarse but not pureed and stir in the milk, eggs, and butter. Stir the liquid ingredients into the dry ingredients just until blended, about 20 strokes; do not overmix. Spoon the mixture into the muffin cups, dividing it evenly.

To make the streusel topping, in a small bowl, stir the brown sugar, flour, and cinnamon together. Add the butter and mix until crumbly. Sprinkle the muffin cups evenly with the streusel mixture and gently pat it down onto the top of the batter.

Bake for 20 to 25 minutes, until a wooden skewer inserted in the center of a muffin comes out clean and dry. Cool 1 minute, then remove from the muffin tin and transfer to a wire rack to cool or to a basket to serve warm.

Makes 12 muffins

PER MUFFIN: 201 cal. (26% from fat), 5.9 g. fat, 1 g. fiber

Raspberry Cornmeal Muffins

If you use frozen berries, add them to the batter unthawed and increase the baking time by 5 to 8 minutes.

1½ cups all-purpose flour
¾ cup yellow cornmeal
½ cup plus 1 tablespoon sugar
4 teaspoons baking powder
½ teaspoon salt
1 cup fresh or frozen unthawed raspberries

1 cup skim milk
2 large egg whites, lightly beaten
1 teaspoon vanilla extract
4 tablespoons (½ stick) unsalted butter, melted

Preheat the oven to 400° F. Lightly grease 12 regular-sized muffin cups, or coat with nonstick spray.

In a large bowl, stir the flour, cornmeal, ½ cup sugar, baking powder, and salt together until well blended. Measure 2 tablespoons of the mixture in a small bowl and add the raspberries; toss lightly until the raspberries are coated with the flour mixture. Set aside. In a small bowl, mix the milk, egg whites, vanilla, and butter until blended. Stir the liquid ingredients into the dry ingredients just until the dry ingredients are moistened.

Spoon about 2 tablespoons of the batter into each of the muffin cups. Top with the raspberries, dividing them equally. Top with the remaining batter, dividing it evenly. Sprinkle with the remaining 1 tablespoon sugar. Bake for 20 to 25 minutes, until light golden brown and a wooden skewer inserted just off center of a muffin comes out clean. Cool 1 minute, then remove from the muffin tin and transfer to a wire rack to cool or to a basket to serve warm.

Makes 12 muffins

PER MUFFIN: 173 cal. (22% from fat), 4 g. fat, 1.7 g. fiber

Fat-free Muffins

Apricot~Honey Muffins

N̲o fat, but the generous amounts of apricots and honey in these muffins provide lots of flavor and give these guilt-free treats a beautiful, warm color. And, in the quest for the tenderest muffins, these are winners, thanks to the apricot-honey puree. They are lovely for a summer breakfast.

2 cups all-purpose flour	*¹⁄₂ cup honey*
¹⁄₄ cup sugar	*1 cup skim milk*
4 teaspoons baking powder	*1 cup dried apricot puree (see*
¹⁄₂ teaspoon salt	*Note)*
¹⁄₄ teaspoon ground nutmeg	*2 large egg whites, lightly beaten*

Preheat the oven to 400° F. Lightly grease 12 regular-sized muffin cups, or coat with nonstick spray.

In a large bowl, stir together the flour, sugar, baking powder, salt, and nutmeg. In a small bowl, mix the honey, milk, apricot puree, and egg whites.

Stir the liquid ingredients into the dry ingredients just until blended, about 25 strokes.

Spoon the batter into the muffin cups, dividing the batter evenly among the cups. Bake for 20 to 25 minutes, or until the muffins are lightly browned and a wooden skewer inserted in the center of a muffin comes out clean. Cool 1 minute, then remove from the muffin tin and transfer to a wire rack to cool or to a basket to serve warm.

Makes 12 muffins

PER MUFFIN: 171 cal., less than 1 g. fat, 1.41 g. fiber

NOTE: To make the apricot puree, combine 1 cup dried apricots and $\frac{1}{2}$ cup water in a saucepan; bring to a boil over medium-high heat. Reduce the heat and simmer for 8 minutes, or until most of the liquid has boiled away. Place in a blender or in a food processor and process until pureed. Cool.

Applesauce-Blueberry Muffins

Applesauce is a fantastic way to make baked goods moist while cutting down on oils and fats. Here fats are completely eliminated because these muffins are also made with skim milk and egg whites only.

1½ cups all-purpose flour
½ cup plus 1 tablespoon wheat germ
¼ cup sugar
3 teaspoons baking powder
½ teaspoon salt
1 teaspoon ground cinnamon

1 cup fresh blueberries, washed
½ cup light corn syrup
¾ cup skim milk
1 cup unsweetened applesauce
1 cup bran flakes, slightly crushed

Preheat the oven to 400° F. Lightly grease 12 regular-sized muffin cups, or coat with nonstick spray.

In a large mixing bowl, combine the flour, ½ cup wheat germ, sugar, baking powder, salt, cinnamon, and blueberries.

In a small bowl, mix the corn syrup, milk, applesauce, bran flakes, and egg whites. Stir the liquid ingredients into the dry ingredients just until the dry ingredients are moistened, about 20 strokes.

Spoon the batter into the muffin cups, dividing the batter evenly.

Sprinkle the remaining tablespoon of wheat germ evenly over the muffins. Pat down gently onto the muffins. Bake for 20 to 25 minutes, or until the muffins are browned and a wooden skewer inserted in the center of a muffin comes out clean. Cool 1 minute, then remove from the muffin tin and transfer to a wire rack to cool or to a basket to serve warm.

Makes 12 muffins

PER MUFFIN: 157 cal., 0 g. fat, 2 g. fiber

Brown-Bread Muffins

These muffins are so quick and easy to make and contain ingredients that store well, such as the buttermilk powder, which is available in the baking section of the supermarket and very useful to have on hand. Whole wheat flour contains a small amount of oil, which accounts for the trace amount of fat in these muffins.

2 cups whole wheat flour
⅔ cup all-purpose flour
½ cup packed brown sugar
2 teaspoons baking soda
½ teaspoon salt

1 teaspoon pumpkin pie spice
2 cups nonfat buttermilk, or 2 cups water mixed with 5 tablespoons buttermilk powder
1 cup dark raisins

Preheat the oven to 400° F. Lightly grease 12 regular-sized muffin cups, or coat with nonstick spray.

In a large bowl, stir the flours, brown sugar, baking soda, salt, and pumpkin pie spice together. Add the buttermilk to the dry ingredients and stir until almost moistened, about 15 strokes. Stir in the raisins until just blended.

Spoon the batter into the muffin cups, dividing the batter evenly. Bake for 18 to 22 minutes, or until a wooden skewer inserted in the center of a muffin comes out clean. Immediately remove from the muffin tin and serve warm.

Makes 12 muffins

PER MUFFIN: 174 cal., less than 1 g. fat, 3.3 g. fiber

Cinnamon-Prune Muffins

Pureed prunes replace the fat in these rich, dark muffins that have a hint of maple flavor as well.

2 cups all-purpose flour
1/4 cup sugar
3 teaspoons baking powder
1/2 teaspoon salt
1 teaspoon ground cinnamon
1/2 cup maple syrup
3/4 cup skim milk

1 cup unsweetened prune puree
  (see Note)
2 large egg whites, lightly beaten

WHEAT GERM TOPPING II
1 tablespoon wheat germ
1 tablespoon brown sugar
1/2 teaspoon ground cinnamon

Preheat the oven to 400° F. Lightly grease 12 regular-sized muffin cups, or coat with nonstick spray.

In a large bowl, stir together the flour, sugar, baking powder, salt, and cinnamon. In a small bowl, mix the maple syrup, milk, prune puree, and egg whites. Stir the liquid ingredients into the dry ingredients just until blended, about 25 strokes.

Spoon the batter into the muffin cups, dividing it equally among the cups. For the topping, in a small bowl, mix the wheat germ, brown sugar, and cinnamon. Sprinkle the tops of the muffins with the wheat germ mixture. Bake for 20 to 25 minutes, or until the muffins are lightly browned and a wooden skewer inserted in the center of a muffin comes out clean. Cool 1 minute, then remove from the muffin tin and transfer to a wire rack to cool or to a basket to serve warm.

Makes 12 muffins

PER MUFFIN: 165 cal., less than 1 g. fat, 1.6 g. fiber

NOTE: To make the prune puree, combine 1 cup pitted prunes and $\frac{1}{2}$ cup water in a saucepan. Bring to a boil over medium-high heat, reduce the heat, and simmer for 8 minutes (most of the liquid will boil away). Place the prunes in a blender or a food processor and process until pureed. Cool.

Pumpkin Bran Muffins

These spicy muffins taste like pumpkin pie, and even without added fat, they have a tender texture that can be attributed to the combination of pureed pumpkin and corn syrup. The tiny amount of fat in these muffins comes from the wheat germ.

1¾ cups all-purpose flour
¼ cup wheat germ
½ cup sugar
3 teaspoons baking powder
½ teaspoon salt
1½ teaspoons pumpkin pie spice

2 large egg whites
1 cup fresh or canned pureed cooked pumpkin
1 cup shredded bran cereal
¾ cup skim milk
½ cup dark corn syrup

Preheat the oven to 400° F. Lightly grease 12 regular-sized muffin cups, or coat with nonstick spray.

In a large bowl, mix together the flour, wheat germ, sugar, baking powder, salt, and pumpkin pie spice. In a small bowl, mix together the egg whites, pumpkin, bran cereal, milk, and corn syrup. Add the liquid ingredients to the dry ingredients and stir just until the dry ingredients are moistened, about 20 strokes.

Spoon the batter into the muffin cups, dividing the batter evenly. Bake for 20 to 25 minutes, or until the muffins feel firm and a wooden skewer inserted in the center of a muffin comes out clean. Cool 1 minute, then remove from the muffin tin and transfer to a wire rack to cool or a basket to serve warm.

Makes 12 muffins

PER MUFFIN: 176 cal., less than 1 g. fat, 3 g. fiber

Spiced Bran Muffins

Corn syrup and applesauce add not only great taste and a nice browning quality to these muffins, but a smooth texture as well.

2 cups all-purpose flour
1/3 cup sugar
3 teaspoons baking powder
1/2 teaspoon salt
1 teaspoon ground cinnamon
1/4 teaspoon ground nutmeg
1/8 teaspoon ground cloves

2 large egg whites, lightly beaten
1 cup unsweetened applesauce
1 cup bran flakes, slightly
    crushed
3/4 cup skim milk
1/2 cup light corn syrup

Preheat the oven to 400° F. Lightly grease 12 regular-sized muffin cups, or coat with nonstick spray.

In a large bowl, mix together the flour, sugar, baking powder, salt, cinnamon, nutmeg, and cloves.

In a small bowl, mix together the egg whites, applesauce, bran flakes, milk, and corn syrup. Add the liquid ingredients to the dry ingredients and stir until mixed, about 25 strokes.

Spoon the batter into the muffin cups, dividing the batter evenly. Bake for 20 to 25 minutes, or until the muffins are browned and a wooden skewer inserted in the center of a muffin comes out clean. Cool 1 minute, then remove from the muffin tin and transfer to a wire rack to cool or to a basket to serve warm.

Makes 12 muffins

PER MUFFIN: 167 cal., less than 1 g. fat, 1.4 g. fiber

English-Muffin Muffins

This muffin should eliminate any baker's fear of baking with yeast. Fast-rising yeast makes these light and delicious muffins as easy as any quick bread. There's no special handling of the yeast because it is measured into the flour mixture just like the other dry ingredients. After the muffin dough is mixed and spooned into the muffin pans, the muffins are left to rise at room temperature for about 30 minutes.

Yeast-raised muffins are tender without any added fat, and they're irresistible fresh out of the oven spread with light or nonfat cream cheese and homemade strawberry jam.

2½ cups all-purpose flour
1 package (2¾ teaspoons) quick-rising yeast
1 tablespoon sugar

1 teaspoon salt
1½ cups very warm (about 135° F.) skim milk

Lightly grease 12 regular-sized muffin cups, or coat with nonstick spray.

In a large mixing bowl, stir together the flour, yeast, sugar, and salt. Add the milk and beat with a wooden spoon until the mixture is smooth and elastic, about 3 minutes.

Spoon the mixture into the muffin cups, dividing it equally. Let the dough rest uncovered for 30 minutes, or until it fills the muffin cups.

Preheat the oven to 400° F.

Bake for 20 minutes, or until a wooden skewer inserted in the center of a muffin comes out clean. Cool 1 minute, then remove from the muffin tin and transfer to a wire rack to cool or to a basket to serve warm.

Makes 12 muffins

PER MUFFIN: 110 cal., less than 1 g. fat, 1 g. fiber

HERBED ENGLISH-MUFFIN MUFFINS: Add 1 tablespoon mixed Italian herbs to the dry ingredients before adding the milk.

SUN-DRIED TOMATO AND BLACK OLIVE ENGLISH-MUFFIN MUFFINS: These will add a little fat to the basic recipe, but not much. Add ½ cup chopped well-drained oil-packed sun-dried tomatoes and 1 cup chopped black olives to the dry ingredients before adding the milk.

WHEATED ENGLISH-MUFFIN MUFFINS: Replace 1 cup of the all-purpose flour with whole wheat flour.

Three-Grain Honey and Fruit Muffins

Healthy tasting, these are ideal for serving with a chunky vegetable soup. Honey brings out the whole-grain flavors, and dried fruits provide a sweet flavor and chewy texture.

1 cup whole wheat flour
1/2 cup all-purpose flour
1/2 cup unsifted dark stone-ground rye flour
1/2 cup old-fashioned rolled oats
3 teaspoons baking powder
1/2 teaspoon baking soda
1/2 teaspoon salt

2 cups nonfat buttermilk, or 2 cups water mixed with 1/2 cup nonfat buttermilk powder
2 egg whites, lightly beaten
1/2 cup honey
1 cup chopped mixed dried fruits, chopped dates, or raisins

Preheat the oven to 400° F. Lightly grease 12 regular-sized muffin cups, or coat with nonstick spray.

In a large mixing bowl, stir together the whole wheat flour, all-purpose flour, rye flour, rolled oats, baking powder, baking soda, and salt. In a medium bowl, mix the buttermilk, egg whites, and honey. Stir the buttermilk mixture into the dry ingredients until the flour mixture is almost moistened. Stir in the fruit just until combined.

Spoon the batter into the muffin cups, dividing the batter evenly. Bake for 20 to 25 minutes, or until a wooden skewer inserted in the center of a muffin comes out clean. Cool 1 minute, then remove from the muffin tin and transfer to a wire rack to cool or to a basket to serve warm.

Makes 12 muffins

PER MUFFIN: 151 cal., less than 1 g. fat, 3.3 g. fiber

Savory Muffins

Bell Pepper — Corn Muffins

Although fresh jalapeño peppers pack a lot of heat, they mellow out when they are baked into muffins, leaving just a mild zing. Use plastic gloves when handling the raw peppers.

3 tablespoons corn oil
½ cup chopped and seeded red bell pepper
1 small jalapeño pepper, seeded and chopped
1½ cups all-purpose flour

½ cup yellow cornmeal
4 tablespoons sugar
3 teaspoons baking powder
¾ teaspoon salt
½ cup skim milk
2 large eggs, lightly beaten

Preheat the oven to 400° F. Lightly grease 12 regular-sized muffin cups, or coat with nonstick spray.

In a small nonstick skillet, heat the oil and add the red pepper and jalapeño pepper. Cook over medium heat for 5 minutes, or until the peppers are brightly colored and crisp-tender. Remove them from the heat and cool while preparing the muffin batter.

In a large bowl, stir the flour, cornmeal, sugar, baking powder, and salt together. In a small bowl, combine the milk, eggs, and pepper mixture.

Add the liquid ingredients to the dry ingredients and stir just until combined, about 20 strokes. Spoon the batter into the muffin cups, dividing the batter evenly. Bake for 12 to 18 minutes, or until a wooden skewer inserted in the center of a muffin comes out clean. Cool 1 minute, then remove from the muffin tin and transfer to a wire rack to cool or to a basket to serve warm.

Makes 12 muffins

PER MUFFIN: 141 cal. (29% from fat), 4.52 g. fat, 0.934 g. fiber

Honey — Blue Corn Muffins

Served warm, spread with Fat-free Jalapeño-Orange Preserves (see page 84), these muffins are perfect with a hot bowl of chili or vegetable soup. I buy blue cornmeal at my local whole-foods cooperative.

1 cup all-purpose flour
1 cup blue or yellow cornmeal
3 teaspoons baking powder
½ teaspoon salt
1 cup skim milk

1 large egg, lightly beaten
2 tablespoons honey
2 tablespoons (¼ stick)
* unsalted butter, melted*

Preheat the oven to 400° F. Lightly grease 12 regular-sized muffin cups, or coat with nonstick spray.

In a large bowl, thoroughly mix the flour, cornmeal, baking powder, and salt. In a small bowl, whisk together the milk, egg, honey, and butter. Add the liquid ingredients to the dry ingredients and stir just until the dry ingredients are moistened, about 20 strokes.

Spoon the batter into the muffin cups, dividing the batter evenly. Bake for 15 to 20 minutes, or until a wooden skewer inserted in the center of a muffin comes out clean. Let the muffins cool in the tin for about 3 minutes, remove, and cool on a rack or transfer to a basket to serve warm.

Makes 12 muffins

PER MUFFIN: 121 cal. (20% from fat), 2.6 g. fat, 1.13 g. fiber

Caraway Rye Mini-Muffins

Flavored with caraway, anise, and orange, these muffins have the flavors of Swedish limpa bread. Serve these crunchy little muffins hot with a salad or a hearty soup. The batch is a small one, enough for 3 or 4 people to have 3 or 4 tiny muffins each; you can double it if you like. For this recipe I prefer to use unsifted dark rye flour. Flour that is labeled "light" or "medium" has a powdery texture, and all the good rye bran has been sifted out.

½ cup unsifted stone-ground dark
    rye flour
½ cup all-purpose flour
1 teaspoon baking powder
¼ teaspoon baking soda
¼ teaspoon salt
¼ teaspoon caraway seeds

¼ teaspoon anise seeds
1 teaspoon grated orange zest
½ cup nonfat plain yogurt,
    stirred
1 large egg, lightly beaten
1 tablespoon corn oil
1 tablespoon honey

Preheat the oven to 400° F. Lightly grease 12 miniature muffin cups, or coat with nonstick spray.

In a large bowl, thoroughly mix the rye flour, all-purpose flour, baking powder, baking soda, salt, caraway seeds, anise seeds, and orange zest. In a small bowl, whisk together the yogurt, egg, oil, and honey. Add the liquid ingredients to the dry ingredients and stir just until the dry ingredients are moistened, about 20 strokes.

Spoon the batter into the muffin cups, dividing the batter evenly. Bake for 15 to 20 minutes, or until a wooden skewer inserted in the center of a muffin comes out clean. Let cool in the tin for 2 to 3 minutes, remove, and cool on a rack or transfer to a basket to serve warm.

Makes 12 mini-muffins

PER MUFFIN: 61 cal. (26% from fat), 1.7 g. fat, 0.8 g. fiber

Dilly Cheese Muffins

The moistness of these muffins comes from nonfat cottage cheese. I like to serve them with grilled or broiled salmon.

2 cups all-purpose flour
1 tablespoon sugar
1 tablespoon chopped fresh dill, or
    1 teaspoon dried dill weed
3 teaspoons baking powder
½ teaspoon baking soda

½ teaspoon salt
2 large egg whites, lightly beaten
1 cup skim milk
3 tablespoons unsalted butter,
    melted
¾ cup nonfat cottage cheese

Preheat the oven to 400° F. Lightly grease 12 regular-sized muffin cups, or coat with nonstick spray.

In a large bowl, mix the flour, sugar, dill, baking powder, baking soda, and salt. In a small bowl, mix the egg whites, milk, butter, and cottage cheese. Stir the liquid ingredients into the dry ingredients just until blended, about 20 strokes.

Spoon the batter into the muffin cups, dividing the batter evenly. Bake for 20 to 25 minutes, or until the muffins are lightly browned and a wooden skewer inserted in the center of a muffin comes out clean. Cool 1 minute, then remove from the muffin tin and transfer to a wire rack to cool or to a basket to serve warm.

Makes 12 muffins

PER MUFFIN: 119 cal. (24% from fat), 3 g. fat, 0.5 g. fiber

Rosemary-Parmesan Muffins

Savory muffins particularly challenge the 30% (or less)–calories-from-fat rule, as they don't depend on pureed fruits, which help keep sweet muffins tender. So I tried cake flour, which has two-thirds less gluten than all-purpose flour. Gluten, while an important ingredient in yeast breads, needs to be tenderized with fat and sugar in a quick bread. When I used cake flour, the muffins were tender and light textured with only a small amount of fat needed.

2½ cups sifted cake flour
1 tablespoon sugar
2 teaspoons baking powder
¾ teaspoon baking soda
½ teaspoon salt
2 teaspoons fresh or dried
    rosemary leaves

3 tablespoons extra-virgin olive
    oil
1½ cups nonfat plain yogurt,
    stirred
½ cup freshly grated Parmesan
    cheese

Preheat the oven to 400° F. Lightly grease 12 regular-sized muffin cups, or coat with nonstick spray.

Sift the flour, sugar, baking powder, baking soda, and salt into a large mixing bowl. Stir in the rosemary. Add the olive oil and stir until blended. Gently stir in the yogurt and ¼ cup of the cheese, mixing just until the dry ingredients are moistened, about 20 strokes.

Spoon the batter into the muffin cups, dividing the batter evenly. Sprinkle with the remaining cheese. Bake for 12 to 15 minutes, or until a wooden skewer inserted in the center of a muffin comes out clean. Remove from the tin and serve immediately.

Makes 12 muffins

PER MUFFIN: 154 cal. (28% from fat), 4.7 g. fat, 1 g. fiber

Herbed Biscuit Muffins

Tender biscuits are a challenge to produce with just a little bit of shortening. Cake flour in place of all-purpose flour and a rather high percentage of liquid do the trick, making these muffins tender and biscuitlike. A little sugar brings out the flavor of the herbs, too.

2 cups sifted cake flour
2 tablespoons sugar
1 teaspoon dried thyme leaves
1 teaspoon dried marjoram leaves
½ teaspoon dried sage leaves
1 teaspoon baking powder

¾ teaspoon baking soda
½ teaspoon salt
3 tablespoons corn oil
⅔ cup nonfat buttermilk, or
⅔ cup water mixed with
3 tablespoons buttermilk
powder

Preheat the oven to 400° F. Lightly grease 10 regular-sized muffin cups, or coat with nonstick spray.

In a large bowl, combine the flour, sugar, thyme, marjoram, sage, baking powder, baking soda, and salt. Mix well. Stir in the oil until blended.

Add the buttermilk and stir with a fork just until a soft dough forms, about 20 strokes. Spoon the batter into the muffin cups, dividing the batter evenly. Bake for 12 to 15 minutes, or until golden brown and a wooden skewer inserted in the center of a muffin comes out clean. Serve immediately.

Makes 10 muffins

PER MUFFIN: 150 cal. (27% from fat), 4 g. fat, 1 g. fiber

Salsa-Corn Muffins

These are just the best accompaniment to either a hot and spicy chili or a summertime barbecue.

1 cup all-purpose flour
1 cup yellow cornmeal
2 teaspoons baking powder
½ teaspoon baking soda
½ teaspoon salt
1 teaspoon corn oil
¼ cup finely chopped red onion
¼ cup finely diced red bell pepper
½ cup fresh or frozen and thawed
corn kernels

3 tablespoons diced canned
green chilies
¼ cup sugar
⅔ cup mild, medium, or hot
prepared salsa
2 large egg whites, lightly beaten
4 tablespoons (½ stick) unsalted
butter, melted, or 4 tablespoons
corn oil

Heat the oven to 400° F. Lightly grease 12 regular-sized muffin cups, or coat with nonstick spray.

In a large bowl, mix the flour, cornmeal, baking powder, baking soda, and salt. Heat the corn oil in a heavy nonstick skillet over medium heat, and add the onion and pepper. Cook for 2 minutes, stirring, until the pepper is crisp-tender. Remove from the heat.

In another bowl mix the corn, chilies, sugar, salsa, egg whites, and butter or oil. Add the peppers and onions.

Add the salsa mixture to the flour mixture and stir just until blended; the mixture will be lumpy. Spoon the batter into the muffin cups, dividing the batter evenly. Bake for 20 to 25 minutes, until a wooden skewer inserted in the center of a muffin comes out clean. Cool for 5 minutes, then remove the muffins from the tin and serve warm.

Makes 12 muffins

PER MUFFIN: 149 cal. (29% from fat), 4.9 g. fat, 1.72 g. fiber

Raisin~Soda Bread Muffins

Traditional soda bread is a quick bread that is usually shaped into a round loaf. To make muffins, I've added more buttermilk to the batter, making a moister end product. Try them warm or split and toasted with a fruit-flavored low-fat or nonfat yogurt-cheese spread (see page 88).

1½ cups all-purpose flour
1 cup whole wheat flour
2 tablespoons sugar
2 teaspoons baking powder
½ teaspoon baking soda
½ teaspoon salt
1 tablespoon caraway seeds

2 tablespoons (¼ stick) unsalted butter, at room temperature
1¼ cups nonfat or 1% buttermilk
1 large egg white, lightly beaten
1 cup raisins

Preheat the oven to 400° F. Lightly grease 12 regular-sized muffin cups, or coat with nonstick spray.

In a large bowl, stir the flours, sugar, baking powder, baking soda, salt, and caraway seeds together. Cut in the butter until it is blended into the flour mixture. In a small bowl, mix the buttermilk and egg white.

Add the buttermilk mixture to the dry ingredients and stir just until moistened, 15 to 20 strokes. Stir in the raisins. Spoon the batter into the muffin cups, dividing the batter evenly. Bake for 20 to 25 minutes, or until a wooden skewer inserted in the center of a muffin comes out clean. Immediately remove the muffins from the tin and serve warm.

Makes 12 muffins

PER MUFFIN: 146 cal. (14% from fat), 2 g. fat, 2.4 g. fiber

Sun-dried Tomato
and Spinach Muffins

A touch of sugar brings out the flavor of the tomatoes and spinach in these savory muffins. I serve them along with pasta made with aromatic sautéed wild mushrooms and red and yellow bell peppers, but they're also excellent with a bowl of your favorite soup.

2 cups all-purpose flour
1 tablespoon sugar
3 teaspoons baking powder
½ teaspoon salt
¼ teaspoon freshly ground pepper
1 teaspoon dried basil leaves
1 cup loosely packed shredded spinach

½ cup chopped reconstituted sun-dried tomatoes (see Note)
1 cup skim milk
2 large egg whites, lightly beaten
3 tablespoons extra-virgin olive oil
2 tablespoons freshly grated Asiago or Parmesan cheese

Preheat the oven to 400° F. Lightly grease 12 regular-sized muffin cups, or coat with nonstick spray.

In a large bowl, stir the flour, sugar, baking powder, salt, pepper, basil leaves, spinach, and sun-dried tomatoes together until all the ingredients are thoroughly mixed.

In a small bowl, combine the milk, egg whites, and oil.

Add the liquid ingredients to the dry ingredients and stir just until moistened, about 20 strokes.

Spoon the batter into the muffin cups, dividing the batter evenly. Sprinkle the tops of the muffins with the cheese. Bake for 12 to 18 minutes, or until a wooden skewer inserted in the center of a muffin comes out clean. Cool 1 minute, then remove from the muffin tin and transfer to a wire rack to cool or to a basket to serve warm.

Makes 12 muffins

PER MUFFIN: 120 cal. (29% from fat), 3.8 g. fat, about 1 g. fiber

NOTE: To reconstitute dried tomatoes, place them in a large bowl and pour boiling water over them. Press the tomatoes into the water and let them stand for 10 minutes. Drain the tomatoes well before using.

Sour Cream Dilled Corn Muffins

These crunchy-textured muffins make a great accompaniment to broiled fresh fish.

1 cup all-purpose flour
1 cup stone-ground white or
   yellow cornmeal
1/4 cup sugar
2 teaspoons baking powder
1/2 teaspoon baking soda
1 teaspoon salt

1 cup nonfat sour cream
1 large egg, slightly beaten
3/4 cup fresh or frozen and thawed
   corn kernels
1/4 cup corn oil
1 tablespoon chopped fresh dill, or
   1 teaspoon dried dill weed

Preheat the oven to 400° F. Lightly grease 12 regular-sized muffin cups, or coat with nonstick spray.

In a large bowl, thoroughly mix the flour, cornmeal, sugar, baking powder, baking soda, and salt. In a small bowl, whisk together the sour cream, egg, corn, oil, and dill. Add the liquid ingredients to the dry ingredients and stir just until the dry ingredients are moistened, about 20 strokes.

Spoon the batter into the muffin cups, dividing the batter evenly. Bake for 15 to 20 minutes, or until a wooden skewer inserted in the center of a muffin comes out clean. Let the muffins cool in the tin for about 3 minutes, remove, and cool on a rack or transfer to a basket to serve warm.

Makes 12 muffins

PER MUFFIN: 160 cal. (26% from fat), 4.7 g. fat, 1.7 g. fiber

Dessert Muffins

Banana-Chunk Muffins

Chunks of banana create moist, fruity pockets in these muffins when they are baked. Select bananas that are ripe but still tinged with a bit of green for the best results.

2 cups all-purpose flour
4 tablespoons sugar
3 teaspoons baking powder
½ teaspoon salt
1 cup ½-inch cubes fresh banana
1 cup skim milk
1 large egg, lightly beaten

¼ cup (½ stick) unsalted butter,
   melted

CINNAMON-SUGAR
TOPPING
1 tablespoon sugar
½ teaspoon ground cinnamon

Preheat the oven to 400° F. Lightly grease 12 regular-sized muffin cups, or coat with nonstick spray.

In a large bowl, stir the flour, sugar, baking powder, and salt together until well blended. Add the banana cubes and stir gently until they are evenly distributed in the mixture. In a small bowl, mix the milk, egg, and butter until blended. Stir the liquid ingredients into the dry ingredients just until blended, about 20 strokes.

Spoon the batter into the prepared muffin cups, dividing the batter evenly. To make the topping, mix the sugar with the cinnamon. Sprinkle the tops of the muffins with the cinnamon-sugar mixture. Bake for 20 to 25 minutes, until light golden brown or until a wooden skewer inserted in the center of a muffin comes out clean. Cool 1 minute, then remove from the muffin tin and transfer to a wire rack to cool or to a basket to serve warm.

Makes 12 muffins

PER MUFFIN: 156 cal. (26% from fat), 4.5 g. fat, 0.8 g. fiber

Chocolate Spice Zucchini Muffins

Shredded zucchini provides the moistness, and a bit of fat-free cocoa with the spices intensifies the color and flavor. The nut oil both adds flavor and aroma and tenderizes.

1¾ cups all-purpose flour
⅔ cup sugar
1 teaspoon baking powder
½ teaspoon baking soda
2 teaspoons unsweetened dark cocoa powder
½ teaspoon ground cinnamon
½ teaspoon ground nutmeg
½ teaspoon salt

1 cup shredded, unpeeled zucchini
½ cup nonfat buttermilk
2 tablespoons hazelnut, walnut, or macadamia nut oil
2 tablespoons corn oil
2 large egg whites, lightly beaten
1 teaspoon vanilla extract

Preheat the oven to 400° F. Lightly grease 12 regular-sized muffin cups, or coat with nonstick spray.

In a large bowl, mix the flour, sugar, baking powder, baking soda, cocoa, cinnamon, nutmeg, and salt. In another bowl, combine the zucchini, buttermilk, oils, egg whites, and vanilla. Stir the liquid ingredients into the dry ingredients just until blended, about 25 strokes.

Spoon the batter into the muffin cups, dividing the batter evenly. Bake for 20 to 25 minutes, or until the muffins are lightly browned and a wooden skewer inserted in the center of a muffin comes out clean. Cool 1 minute, then remove from the muffin tin and transfer to a wire rack to cool or to a basket to serve warm.

Makes 12 muffins

PER MUFFIN: 158 cal. (28% from fat), 4.8 g. fat, 0.6 g. fiber

Blueberry-Nutmeg-Cream Muffins

My favorite blueberry muffins are cakelike and loaded with small, fresh wild blueberries. When only the large cultivated berries are available, they'll do. Large, commercially frozen berries are my very last choice because the frozen berries change the temperature of the muffin batter, which means that the baking time has to be increased by 5 to 10 minutes.

2 cups sifted cake flour
½ cup plus 1 tablespoon sugar
1½ teaspoons baking powder
½ teaspoon baking soda
½ teaspoon salt
¼ teaspoon ground nutmeg

2 cups fresh, washed or frozen and partially thawed blueberries
2 large eggs, lightly beaten
3 tablespoons corn oil
1 cup nonfat sour cream

Preheat the oven to 400° F. Lightly grease 12 regular-sized muffin cups, or coat with nonstick spray.

In a mixing bowl, stir together the flour, ½ cup sugar, baking powder, baking soda, salt, and nutmeg. Sprinkle 1 tablespoon of the mixture over the blueberries and mix the berries gently to coat them evenly.

In a small bowl, beat the eggs, oil, and sour cream until well mixed. Pour the liquid ingredients over the dry ingredients and stir just to moisten, about 15 strokes. Fold in the berries.

Spoon the batter into the muffin cups, dividing the batter evenly. Sprinkle the tops of the muffins with the remaining 1 tablespoon sugar. Bake for 18 to 22 minutes, until light golden brown or until a wooden skewer inserted in the center of a muffin comes out clean.

Cool 1 minute, then remove from the muffin tin and transfer to a wire rack to cool or to a basket to serve warm.

Makes 12 muffins

PER MUFFIN: 174 cal. (24% from fat), 4.7 g. fat, 1.13 g. fiber

MINI-MUFFINS: Spoon the batter into 36 miniature greased muffin cups. Bake for 10 to 12 minutes, until golden.

GIANT MUFFINS: Spoon the mixture into 6 large greased muffin cups. Bake for 25 to 30 minutes, or until a wooden skewer inserted in the center of a muffin comes out clean.

Carrot-Applesauce Muffins

These muffins have all the spiciness and richness of carrot cake without the fat.

2½ cups all-purpose flour
¾ cup sugar
2½ teaspoons baking powder
¼ teaspoon baking soda
¼ teaspoon salt
1½ teaspoons ground cinnamon
½ teaspoon ground ginger
¼ teaspoon ground nutmeg
⅛ teaspoon ground cloves

1½ cups finely shredded carrots
½ cup nonfat plain yogurt
1 large egg, lightly beaten
¼ cup safflower or vegetable oil
1 teaspoon vanilla extract
1 cup unsweetened applesauce
1 tablespoon flaked sweetened coconut

Preheat the oven to 400° F. Lightly grease 12 regular-sized muffin cups, or coat with nonstick spray.

In a large mixing bowl, combine the flour, sugar, baking powder, baking soda, salt, cinnamon, ginger, nutmeg, and cloves. Add the shredded carrots and mix until blended into the dry ingredients.

In a small bowl, stir together the yogurt, egg, oil, vanilla extract, and applesauce. Stir the liquid ingredients into the dry ingredients just until the dry ingredients are moistened, about 20 strokes.

Spoon the batter into the muffin cups. Sprinkle each muffin with a pinch of coconut. Pat the coconut gently onto the muffins. Bake for 20 to 22 minutes, or until a wooden skewer inserted in the center of a muffin comes out clean. Cool 1 minute, then remove from the muffin tin and transfer to a rack to cool or a basket to serve warm.

Makes 12 muffins

PER MUFFIN: 232 cal. (21% from fat), 5.34 g. fat, 1.86 g. fiber

Fresh Raspberry Muffins

These are the best with fresh raspberries because frozen raspberries turn watery and streak the muffins as they thaw. The crinkly top comes from a bit of extra sugar that I sprinkle over each muffin to make it more "dessert."

2 cups all-purpose flour
½ cup plus 1 tablespoon sugar
3 teaspoons baking powder
½ teaspoon salt
1 teaspoon grated orange zest
1 cup fresh raspberries

¾ cup skim milk
5 tablespoons unsalted butter, melted
1 large egg, lightly beaten
1 large egg white, lightly beaten

Preheat the oven to 400° F. Lightly grease 12 regular-sized muffin cups, or coat with nonstick spray.

In a mixing bowl, stir together the flour, ½ cup sugar, baking powder, salt, and orange zest. Sprinkle 1 tablespoon of the mixture over the raspberries and mix the berries gently to coat them evenly.

In a small bowl, combine the milk, butter, egg, and egg white. Pour the liquid ingredients over the dry ingredients and stir just to moisten, about 20 strokes. Fold in the berries.

Spoon the batter into the muffin cups, dividing the batter evenly. Sprinkle the tops of the muffins with the remaining 1 tablespoon sugar. Bake for 20 to 25 minutes, or until light golden brown and a wooden skewer inserted in the center of a muffin comes out clean. Cool 1 minute, then remove from the muffin tin and transfer to a wire rack to cool or to a basket to serve warm.

Makes 12 muffins

PER MUFFIN: 172 cal. (29% from fat), 5.5 g. fat, 1.2 g. fiber

Gingerbread Muffins
with Lemon Sauce

The batter for these spicy dessert muffins is quick to stir up. I usually have all the ingredients right on the cupboard shelf. Sometimes I serve them as I do gingerbread, topped with whipped cream and sliced fresh strawberries. But when I'm cutting fat, I don't feel deprived with this delicious, tart lemon sauce, which is smoothed with just a tablespoon of butter for 12 servings.

2 cups all-purpose flour	*LEMON SAUCE*
1 tablespoon pumpkin pie spice	½ cup sugar
1 teaspoon baking soda	1 tablespoon cornstarch
½ teaspoon salt	⅛ teaspoon salt
1 cup light molasses	1 cup boiling water
¼ cup packed brown sugar	1 tablespoon unsalted butter
⅓ cup safflower or corn oil	1 teaspoon grated lemon zest
1 cup boiling water	3 tablespoons lemon juice

Preheat the oven to 400° F. Lightly grease 12 regular-sized muffin cups, or coat with nonstick spray.

In a medium bowl, sift the flour, pumpkin pie spice, baking soda, and salt together. In a large bowl, mix the molasses, brown sugar, and oil. Pour the boiling water into the molasses mixture and beat with a mixer or a whisk until the brown sugar is dissolved. Add the flour mixture and mix just until all the lumps of flour are dissolved in the batter, about 20 strokes.

Spoon the batter into the muffin cups, dividing the batter evenly. Bake for 20 minutes, or until the muffins are lightly browned or until a wooden skewer inserted in the center of a muffin comes out clean.

While muffins bake, make the lemon sauce. In a medium saucepan, combine the sugar, cornstarch, and salt. Slowly stir in the boiling water. Place over medium heat and cook for 5 minutes, stirring until thickened. Remove from the heat and stir in the butter, lemon zest, and lemon juice.

Cool the muffins for 1 minute before removing from the tin to serve. Serve warm with 2 tablespoons lemon sauce spooned over each muffin.

Makes 12 muffins

PER MUFFIN (WITH 2 TABLESPOONS SAUCE): 246 cal. (26% from fat), 7 g. fat, 0.6 g. fiber

Hazelnut-Chocolate Muffins

A few toasted nuts sprinkled on top of these muffins, combined with a nut oil in the batter, make these muffins taste as if they were stuffed with nuts! Hazelnut oil is available in gourmet food stores and in well-stocked, large supermarkets. Made with corn oil, the nut flavor is missing, but the chocolate flavor is pleasing.

¼ cup whole hazelnuts (filberts)
1 cup all-purpose flour
¾ cup whole wheat flour
2 teaspoons baking powder
½ teaspoon baking soda
½ teaspoon salt
½ cup sugar
⅓ cup unsweetened dark cocoa powder

2 teaspoons espresso coffee powder
1 large egg, lightly beaten
2 large egg whites, lightly beaten
1 cup skim milk
2 teaspoons vanilla extract
3 tablespoons hazelnut, walnut, or corn oil

Preheat the oven to 350° F. Spread the nuts on a cookie sheet and toast for 5 to 8 minutes, until the nuts are lightly browned. Remove from the oven and rub the nuts in a towel to remove most of the skins. Chop in a food processor until coarse and set aside. Reset the oven to 400° F. Lightly grease 12 regular-sized muffin cups, or coat with nonstick spray.

In a medium bowl, stir together the flours, baking powder, baking soda, salt, sugar, cocoa powder, and coffee powder.

In a separate bowl, mix the egg, egg whites, milk, vanilla, and oil. Stir the liquid ingredients into the flour mixture just until the dry ingredients are moistened, about 20 strokes. Spoon the batter into the muffin cups, dividing the batter evenly. Sprinkle the toasted nuts over the tops of the muffins. Bake for 15 to 20 minutes, or until lightly browned and a wooden skewer inserted in the center of a muffin comes out clean. Cool 1 minute, then remove from the muffin tin and transfer to a wire rack to cool or to a basket to serve warm.

Makes 12 muffins

PER MUFFIN: 175 cal. (29% from fat), 5 g. fat, 1.65 g. fiber

Strawberry Streusel Muffins

Each one of these muffins is like a miniature coffee cake, with a top that my friend Dexter Larson, who is a wonderful baking instructor, calls a Dutchy crust. This crunchy topping is one that Dutch bakers use for yeast breads, as well as coffee cakes and muffins.

2 cups all-purpose flour
½ cup sugar
3 teaspoons baking powder
1 teaspoon salt
1 cup fresh, washed strawberries, diced into ½-inch pieces
1 cup skim milk
4 tablespoons (½ stick) unsalted butter, melted, or 4 tablespoons corn oil

1 large egg, lightly beaten

STREUSEL TOPPING IV
½ cup all-purpose flour
¼ cup packed brown sugar
2 tablespoons (¼ stick) unsalted butter, melted

Preheat the oven to 400° F. Lightly grease 12 regular-sized muffin cups, or coat with nonstick spray.

In a mixing bowl, stir together the flour, sugar, baking powder, and salt. Sprinkle 1 tablespoon of the mixture over the strawberries and mix the berries gently to coat them evenly.

In a small bowl, combine the milk, butter or corn oil, and egg. Pour the liquid ingredients over the dry ingredients and stir just to moisten, about 15 strokes. Fold in the berries.

Spoon the batter into the muffin cups, dividing the batter evenly. To make the topping, in a small bowl, mix the flour and brown sugar until well blended. Add the 2 tablespoons butter and stir until the mixture makes large, moist crumbs. Sprinkle the tops of the muffins with the crumb mixture and press the topping gently into each muffin. Bake for 20 to 25 minutes, or until light golden brown and a wooden skewer inserted in the center of a muffin comes out clean. Cool 1 minute, then remove from the muffin tin and transfer to a wire rack to cool or to a basket to serve warm.

Makes 12 muffins

PER MUFFIN: 210 cal. (28% from fat), 6.5 g. fat, 1 g. fiber

Lemon ~ Ginger Muffins

I t's a pleasant surprise to bite into a bit of crystallized ginger in these lemon-scented muffins. Crystallized ginger is available in the gourmet or produce section of most major supermarkets, and I keep it on hand because I love to eat it like candy.

2 cups all-purpose flour
2 teaspoons baking powder
1/4 teaspoon salt
5 tablespoons unsalted butter, softened
2/3 cup sugar

4 teaspoons finely chopped crystallized ginger
2 large eggs, lightly beaten
1 teaspoon grated lemon zest
1 cup skim milk

Preheat the oven to 400° F. Lightly grease 12 regular-sized muffin cups, or coat with nonstick spray.

In a medium bowl, stir together the flour, baking powder, and salt. In a large bowl, cream the butter and sugar together with an electric mixer until blended. Add the ginger and eggs and beat until light and fluffy. Add the lemon zest. Add the flour mixture and milk to the bowl and stir just until the flour is moistened, about 20 strokes.

Spoon the batter into the muffin cups, dividing the batter evenly. Bake for 15 to 20 minutes, or until lightly browned and a wooden skewer inserted in the center of a muffin comes out clean. Cool 1 minute, then remove from the muffin tin and transfer to a wire rack to cool or to a basket to serve warm.

Makes 12 muffins

PER MUFFIN: 180 cal. (29% from fat), 5.8 g. fat, 0.5 g. fiber

Spreads

Fat-free Fresh Berry Jam

When I have just a small amount of berries—like the wild strawberries we pick in the meadow near our house, or a small carton of blackberries from the grocery store—I like to make this quick fresh-tasting jam. Because this makes just a cup of jam and we use it right away, I don't seal it as I do when making large amounts of preserves. It's irresistible served when the jam is still a little warm from cooking.

1 cup fresh strawberries or other berries, washed

¾ cup sugar
1 teaspoon lemon juice

To cook in a microwave, combine the berries, sugar, and lemon juice in a glass bowl. Mash the berries into the sugar and stir until the sugar is dissolved. Cook in the microwave, uncovered, at high power for 5 minutes. Stir and scrape down the sides of the bowl. Microwave for 1 to 3 minutes longer, or until thickened (mixture should reach 218° F. on an instant-reading thermometer).

For stove-top cooking, combine the berries, sugar, and lemon juice in a nonaluminum saucepan. Cook over medium-high heat, stirring constantly, until the mixture comes to a boil. Boil for 5 to 8 minutes, until thickened.

Pour the jam into a serving dish.

Makes about 1 cup

PER SERVING (1 TABLESPOON): 40 cal., 0 g. fat, 0.3 g. fiber

Quick No-fat Apple and Apricot Preserves

Here's another delectable spread that you can make in just minutes, using the microwave or a saucepan, whichever is most convenient.

1 cup chopped fresh apricots	1 cup sugar
1 large Granny Smith apple, peeled, cored, and chopped	½ cup water
	1 3-inch cinnamon stick

Combine all of the ingredients in a 1-quart glass bowl, for the microwave, or in a 2-quart saucepan, for the stove top. Microwave the mixture in the glass bowl for 10 minutes, at high power, stirring once or twice while cooking. Or, heat the mixture in the saucepan to boiling and cook, stirring frequently, for about 10 minutes, or until the mixture is reduced to 2 cups.

Cool, then turn the mixture into a serving dish or a jar. Serve at room temperature. Store, tightly covered, in the refrigerator, for up to 6 weeks.

Makes 2 cups

PER SERVING (1 TABLESPOON): 35 cal., 0 g. fat, 0 g. fiber

Fat~free Jalapeño~ Orange Preserves

I like to keep jars of these preserves on hand to serve with light cream cheese and muffins or crackers for a quick snack. It makes a great gift, too, packed with some ready-baked Honey–Blue Corn Muffins (see page 57) in a pretty basket. Don't try to double or halve this recipe: the cooking times given are just right for these ingredient amounts. On properly sealed canning jars, the jar lids should pop inward, rather than remain convex. You can keep unsealed preserves refrigerated for up to 6 months.

¾ cup finely chopped, green bell pepper
¼ cup finely chopped, seeded, and stemmed jalapeño peppers
1 dried ancho chili pepper, seeded and cut into ¼-inch dice

2 tablespoons grated orange zest
6 cups sugar
1½ cups white vinegar
1 bottle (6 ounces) liquid pectin

Place six 8-ounce canning jars, lids, and rings into a large pot. Add water to cover the jars by 2 inches; heat to boiling and boil the jars and lids for 20 minutes. Reduce the heat to simmering while preparing the preserves.

In a 4-quart saucepan, combine the green peppers, jalapeño peppers, ancho pepper, orange zest, sugar, and vinegar. Heat to boiling. Boil for 1 minute, stirring to prevent the mixture from boiling over. Remove from the heat.

Add the pectin and stir to mix well. Let the preserves stand for 5 minutes. Skim off the white film that forms on top.

With a pair of tongs, remove the jars from the boiling water. Pour the preserves into the hot sterilized jars, dividing them equally.

With a damp cloth, wipe the rims of the jars to remove any preserves. Remove the jar lids and rings from the boiling water and place them on top of the jars, fastening them securely. Cool on a rack. As the preserves cool, the lids will invert when they seal. Refrigerate any jars that did not seal, and use within 6 months.

Makes six 8-ounce jars of preserves

PER SERVING (1 TABLESPOON): 36 cal., 0 g. fat, 0 g. fiber

Fat-free Spicy Pumpkin Butter

I like to spread whole-grain muffins, like cracked wheat and rye, or whole wheat muffins with nonfat or low-fat cream cheese, then top them off with pumpkin butter; the combination tastes like pumpkin pie.

1 cup fresh or canned pureed cooked pumpkin	¼ teaspoon ground nutmeg
	¼ teaspoon ground ginger
1 cup sugar	⅛ teaspoon ground cloves
1 teaspoon ground cinnamon	2 tablespoons lemon juice

Stir the pumpkin, sugar, cinnamon, nutmeg, ginger, cloves, and lemon juice together in a glass bowl for the microwave or in a nonreactive saucepan for the stove top. Cook the mixture in the glass bowl in the microwave oven at high power for 5 minutes, stirring twice. Or, in the saucepan over medium-high heat, stir the mixture until it comes to a boil, then boil 5 minutes, stirring constantly. Cool, then turn the pumpkin butter into a serving dish and serve immediately with fresh, hot muffins. Store, refrigerated, for 4 to 6 weeks.

Makes about 1¼ cups

PER SERVING (1 TABLESPOON): 40 cal., 0 g. fat, 0 g. fiber

Fat-free Three-Minute Blueberry Jam

With just a cup of berries, a bit of sugar, and 3 minutes' cooking in the microwave, you can serve fresh blueberry jam with your favorite breakfast muffin.

1 cup fresh or frozen and thawed unsweetened blueberries

½ cup sugar
1 tablespoon lemon juice

To make in a microwave, in a 1-quart glass bowl, combine the berries, sugar, and lemon juice. Stir to coat the berries with the sugar. Microwave at high power for 3 minutes, stirring halfway through the cooking time.

To cook on the stove top, combine the ingredients in a 1-quart saucepan. Heat to boiling and boil for 3 minutes, stirring often.

Pour into a serving dish, or cool and store, covered, in the refrigerator, 4 to 6 weeks.

Makes 1 cup

PER SERVING (1 TABLESPOON): 40 cal., 0 g. fat, 0 g. fiber

Low-Fat Yogurt Cheese Spread

Rich and creamy yogurt cheese is an ideal substitute for cream cheese or sour cream in spreads for both sweet and savory muffins.

You can make your own yogurt cheese by simply draining the whey from low-fat yogurt through a filter. I have a special reusable plastic filter, available in specialty cookware shops and some cookware catalogs, that works very well. You can also use several thicknesses of cheesecloth or a coffee filter to drain the yogurt. The process usually takes 12 to 24 hours.

There are several flavor variations possible, and you might invent your own. The nutritional calculation is based simply on the basic low-fat yogurt's value.

1 cup low-fat or fruit-flavored plain yogurt

Flavoring of choice (see variations on page 89)

Line a strainer with 4 thicknesses of dampened, clean cheesecloth or with a coffee filter. Spoon the yogurt into the lined strainer. Place over a bowl and cover with plastic wrap. Refrigerate 12 to 24 hours. Discard the drained liquid.

Turn the yogurt cheese into a bowl and stir in the desired flavoring ingredients. Serve as a spread for sweet or savory muffins. The spread will keep, covered, in the refrigerator for 3 days.

Makes about ½ cup

PER SERVING (1 TABLESPOON): 18 cal. (22% from fat), 0.4 g. fat, 0 g. fiber

SAVORY VEGETABLE SPREAD: Stir 2 tablespoons finely shredded carrots, 2 tablespoons finely chopped unpeeled radishes, 1 tablespoon chopped green onions, ⅛ teaspoon salt, and 1 small, mashed garlic clove into the yogurt cheese.

PEPPERED CHIVE-AND-DILL SPREAD: Stir 1 tablespoon finely chopped chives, 1 teaspoon chopped fresh dill, ½ teaspoon coarsely ground black pepper, and ⅛ teaspoon salt into the yogurt cheese.

HERB CHEESE: Stir 4 to 6 tablespoons finely chopped fresh herbs, such as parsley, cilantro, savory, dill, marjoram leaves, chervil, or chives, or a combination of two or more, and salt and pepper to taste into the yogurt cheese.

Turkish Apricot Butter

Turkish apricots are small whole, pitted dried apricots. Quickly cooked and pureed, this spread works deliciously with any breakfast or snack muffin.

1 cup (about 30) packed dried Turkish apricots	½ cup sugar
1 cup water	1 teaspoon unsalted butter

Combine the apricots, water, and sugar in a 1-quart glass bowl, for microwaving, or in a 1-quart saucepan, for stove-top cooking. Microwave the mixture in the glass bowl for 10 minutes, stirring once halfway through the cooking. Or heat the mixture in the saucepan to boiling and cook, stirring, for 10 minutes.

Turn the cooked mixture into a food processor or blender and process until smooth. Add the butter while the motor is going.

Pour the mixture into a serving dish or cool and pour into a jar. Store, covered, for up to 5 months in the refrigerator.

Makes 1¼ cups

PER SERVING (1 TABLESPOON): 36 cal., trace fat, 0 g. fiber

Acknowledgments

I was chatting with my editor, Katie Workman, at Clarkson Potter, when she suggested, "Why not a book on light or low-fat muffins?" I thought it was a great idea, although I knew what the challenge would be. Thank you, Katie!

I'm grateful to both *Cooking Light* and *Fast and Healthy* magazines for giving me the opportunity to face similar low-fat baking challenges in the past. As I worked on these recipes, this little ditty came to my mind:

A muffin that's light is low fat.
Cut out the fat, that's that!
Go too far and it's chewy
and almost too gooey.
The recipe's a balancing act.

Thanks go to my tasters, husband, Richard, plus family and friends who evaluated and passed the final flavors and textures of all of the muffins.

Hearty thanks also to Elise Simon Goodman, my encouraging friend and agent, and her husband, Arnold, for tireless work on my behalf.

And thanks to Renato Stanisic, Andrea Peabbles, Allison Hanes, and everyone at Clarkson Potter for their work on the book.

Index

92

Conversion Chart
Equivalent Imperial and Metric Measurements

American cooks use standard containers, the 8-ounce cup and a tablespoon that takes exactly 16 level fillings to fill that cup level. Measuring by cup makes it very difficult to give weight equivalents, as a cup of densely packed butter will weigh considerably more than a cup of flour. The easiest way therefore to deal with cup measurements in recipes is to take the amount by volume rather than by weight. Thus the equation reads:

1 cup = 240 ml = 8 fl. oz.   ½ cup = 120 ml = 4 fl. oz.

It is possible to buy a set of American cup measures in major stores around the world.

In the States, butter is often measured in sticks. One stick is the equivalent of 8 tablespoons. One tablespoon of butter is therefore the equivalent to ½ ounce/15 grams.

LIQUID MEASURES

Fluid Ounces	U.S.	Imperial	Milliliters
	1 teaspoon	1 teaspoon	5
¼	2 teaspoons	1 dessertspoon	10
½	1 tablespoon	1 tablespoon	14
1	2 tablespoons	2 tablespoons	28
2	¼ cup	4 tablespoons	56
4	½ cup		110
5		¼ pint or 1 gill	140
6	¾ cup		170
8	1 cup		225
9			250, ¼ liter
10	1¼ cups	½ pint	280
12	1½ cups		340
15		¾ pint	420
16	2 cups		450
18	2¼ cups		500, ½ liter
20	2½ cups	1 pint	560
24	3 cups		675
25		1¼ pints	700
27	3½ cups		750
30	3¾ cups	1½ pints	840
32	4 cups or 1 quart		900
35		1¾ pints	980
36	4½ cups		1000, 1 liter
40	5 cups	2 pints or 1 quart	1120

SOLID MEASURES

U.S. and Imperial Measures		Metric Measures	
Ounces	Pounds	Grams	Kilos
1		28	
2		56	
3½		100	
4	¼	112	
5		140	
6		168	
8	½	225	
9		250	¼
12	¾	340	
16	1	450	
18		500	½
20	1¼	560	
24	1½	675	
27		750	¾
28	1¾	780	
32	2	900	
36	2¼	1000	1
40	2½	1100	
48	3	1350	
54		1500	1½

OVEN TEMPERATURE EQUIVALENTS

Fahrenheit	Celsius	Gas Mark	Description
225	110	¼	Cool
250	130	½	
275	140	1	Very Slow
300	150	2	
325	170	3	Slow
350	180	4	Moderate
375	190	5	
400	200	6	Moderately Hot
425	220	7	Fairly Hot
450	230	8	Hot
475	240	9	Very Hot
500	250	10	Extremely Hot

Any broiling recipes can be used with the grill of the oven, but beware of high-temperature grills.

EQUIVALENTS FOR INGREDIENTS

all-purpose flour—plain flour
coarse salt—kitchen salt
cornstarch—cornflour
eggplant—aubergine

half and half—12% fat milk
heavy cream—double cream
light cream—single cream
lima beans—broad beans

scallion—spring onion
unbleached flour—strong, white flour
zest—rind
zucchini—courgettes or marrow